Macro Diet Cookbook for Beginners

Discover Your Energy Balance with 400 Flavorful and Easy Recipes.

Embrace a New Way of Living with a Flexible 4-Weeks Meal Plan to Burn Fat and Gain Lean Muscle

Kendall Anderson

© **Copyright 2021 - All rights reserved.**

The content contained within this book may not be reproduced, duplicated or transmitted without direct written permission from the author or the publisher.

Under no circumstances will any blame or legal responsibility be held against the publisher, or author, for any damages, reparation, or monetary loss due to the information contained within this book, either directly or indirectly.

Legal Notice:

This book is copyright protected. It is only for personal use. You cannot amend, distribute, sell, use, quote or paraphrase any part, or the content within this book, without the consent of the author or publisher.

Disclaimer Notice:

Please note the information contained within this document is for educational and entertainment purposes only. All effort has been executed to present accurate, up to date, reliable, complete information. No warranties of any kind are declared or implied. Readers acknowledge that the author is not engaged in the rendering of legal, financial, medical or professional advice. The content within this book has been derived from various sources. Please consult a licensed professional before attempting any techniques outlined in this book.

By reading this document, the reader agrees that under no circumstances is the author responsible for any losses, direct or indirect, that are incurred as a result of the use of the information contained within this document, including, but not limited to, errors, omissions, or inaccuracies.

Table of Contents

Table of Contents 3
Introduction 6
What is the Macro Diet? 6
A Brief History 6
How does the Macro Diet Work? 7
What Makes the Macro Diet Different? ... 7
How to Calculate Your Macros 8
How to Use this Cookbook 9
Chapter 1: Understanding the Main Four Food Groups of this Diet 10
Balance and Why it is Key 10
Carbohydrates, Evil or Misunderstood? ... 10
A Note on Gluten 11
Protein, Your Best Friend 11
Dietary Restrictions? No Problem! 11
A Note on Dairy 11
Fats, Not Free 12
Vegetables and Micronutrients 13
Micronutrients vs. Macronutrients 13
Chapter 2: Soups 14
The Mighty Soup 14
Shopping List 15
Recommended Appliances 15
Recommended Ingredients 15
Hot Soups 16

Cold Soups 21
Vegetarian Soups 26
Chapter 3: Salads 31
Salads and why they are Important 31
Dressings 32
Shopping List 32
Protein-Packed Salads 37
Shopping List 37
Vegan/Vegetarian 40
Lighter Salads 42
Chapter 4: Sandwiches and Wraps 47
Sandwiches, Wraps, and Versatility 47
Shopping List 48
Cold Sandwiches 50
Hot Sandwiches 54
Wraps 59
Chapter 5: Poultry 65
The Chicken and the Turkey 65
Stews 67
Grilling 72
Pans and Ovens 75
Chapter 6: Pork 79
Power in Pork 79
Shopping List 80
Stews 81

Grilling	85
Pans and Ovens	88
Chapter 7: Beef	91
The King of Meat	91
A Note on Grilling Steaks	92
Shopping List	92
Stews	93
Grilling	93
Chapter 8: Seafood	95
Gifts from the Sea	95
Grilling	96
Pans and Ovens	97
Chapter 9: Vegetarian and Vegan	98
Vegetables and Their Role	98
Chapter 10: Pizzas and Pasta	102
Italian Delights	102
Making Your Own Dough?	102
Chapter 11: Snacks	103
Snacking and Timing	103
Protein-Packed	105
Fruits and Veggies	108
Sweets	112
Chapter 12: Desserts	117
Delightful Desserts	117
Shopping List	118
Breakfast Desserts	119
Fruit Desserts	123
Dairy Desserts	128
Chapter 13: Two-Week Programs	134
Let's See This in Action!	134
Two-Week Program for Men	134
Two-Week Program for Women	138
Conclusion	142
References	143

Introduction

Diets come in many different forms, each claiming to be better than the last. Often, these diets have a flaw in them that the creator either did not see or did not mention, leading to people failing their diet and/or losing interest and momentum in their regimen. Common failures of other diets include restricting the food you can eat and calorie counting without focusing on nutrition or simply based on intuition and anecdotes instead of proper research from nutritionists and dieticians.

The Macro diet continues to be the best diet to choose for weight loss, weight gain, and health maintenance. It's the only diet that can work long-term by not sacrificing flavor and portion size to reach the optimal benefit.

What is the Macro Diet?

Diets are named for many things such as the person who created them or even when the diet supposedly originated. The Macro diet could have fallen under either of these. Still, the diet's name has persisted throughout millennia, and its historical effectiveness speaks for itself.

A Brief History

The Macro diet gets its name from Macrobiotics, which combines the Greek words 'Macro,' meaning 'great' or 'long,' and 'bios,' which means 'life.' The Greek writer and physician Hippocrates developed the first iteration of the Macro diet. He believed that fresh seasonal food and outdoor exercise were necessary to create more robust and healthier people.

The diet would resurface again in 1796 when Dr. Christoph Wilhelm Hufeland, a famous Prussian physician, published his book Macrobiotics: The Art of Prolonging Life. His primary focus was less on seasonality and more on natural foods, with vegetables taking center stage.

The modern macro diet began with Dr. Sagen Ishizuka of the Japanese Imperial Army. Ishizuka noticed that when western diets were introduced to the Japanese people, there were higher incidences of disease. He focused on simple, natural foods for his patients and helped thousands of Japanese recover their health. His diets consisted of whole grains, sea vegetables, and common Japanese vegetables. Ishizuka's influence is felt all over Japan, as his dietary beliefs persist among Japanese chefs, dieticians, and nutritionists.

In the early 1920s, a man named George Ohsawa coined the term "Macrobiotic diet" after using Ishizuka's methods to recover from a case of tuberculosis which could have ended his life. Ohsawa would become a humanitarian with his story, sharing his food ideas, and his incredible story of recovery. He made the Macro diet a household name around the world.

Ohsawa's work was continued by his students, who further studied his works and the ideas of the effective macro diet. Many of his students include Michio and Aveline Kushi, Cornellia and Herman Aihara, Noburo Muramoto and William Dufty in North America, Roland Yasuhara in Belgium, Clim Yoshimi in France, and, still actively teaching in Brazil, Tomio Kikuchi.

The diet's history and effectiveness genuinely speak for themselves, and the benefits of the diet are felt worldwide to this day. Its influence spreads over academia, thousands of people's lives, and entire countries to achieve the healthiest results.

How does the Macro Diet Work?

The Macro diet focuses on balance, as mentioned above. The diet is meant to focus on four main food groups, carbohydrates, vegetables, proteins, and fats, to create an optimally healthy person. The diet believes in balancing your body and physical activity to make you the healthiest possible individual. Your body is a living and working machine that needs maintenance and fuel to operate at peak capacity. The Macro diet focuses on the fuel aspect to feed the body the nutrients it needs appropriately.

That's not to say the diet lacks flavor. Macro diet foods can be some of the best tasting foods available. The options and the varieties are limitless for those who want to follow this diet. The fact that each meal is balanced for health also means that it's balanced for flavor. Imagine being excited to eat every meal because of how delicious it will be as well as good for you. That's how you'll stick to this diet and do so without any complaints. There are other reasons, too, considering the differences between the Macro diet and other diets.

What Makes the Macro Diet Different?

The goal of the diet is to achieve balance in your diet by focusing on the most critical aspects of the food we eat every day. The Macro diet is also standard in many countries around the world where people are leading happy and healthy lives simply by following the eating traditions of their country. That's not to say you can't benefit from this diet if you don't live in those parts of the world. All you need to do is change how you shop and view food in your area. So long as you have access to a supermarket or can reliably attain their everyday products, a basic kitchen setup, and the desire to see results, you can begin and will benefit from the Macro diet.

The other thing that makes this diet different from the others is that it's not a fad. This is a scientifically proven diet that continues to help people all over the world. It's the only one with consistent results with no negative repercussions for those who decide to pursue it for the sake of their health. Make no mistake: The Macro Diet isn't meant to be a trend. This isn't something you can do for a few months and then tell your friends not to do it after you've abandoned it because you felt it wasn't for you. The Macro diet is accessible for just about anyone on any budget. It is for everyone because there are no restrictions except for those you put on yourself for personal or health reasons. Even in those cases, the Macro diet can be followed because it is so versatile. Even if you're a hardcore vegan, this cookbook is filled with vegan and vegetarian recipes. Even if a recipe calls for an animal product, you should know how to substitute them to create your own version of the dish.

Forget about calorie counting as you know it, too. Every person has different caloric intake needs. It's more important to balance what you're eating rather than count how many calories each meal contains. Caloric values will be mentioned in the recipes, as will portion sizes. Still, these aren't there to measure how many calories you eat. They are there for nutritionists and other health professionals to understand which recipes would work better for their patients on a given day. Generally, it's always best to consult your doctor before starting any diet or exercise regimen so you can identify your needs. The calories are there to help you with those needs rather than restrict your choice of what to eat.

That said, without knowing your physical activity, age, gender, exercise habits, muscle mass, body mass index, supplements taken, genetic factors, weather, and pregnancy status, it's impossible to know the specifics your body needs without consulting your doctor. That doesn't mean that you can't start the macro diet without this information. It just means the ideal way of following the diet for your needs is unknown until you speak to your doctor. Suppose you know your own conditions and limitations. In that case, you can use the formula in the next section to determine your caloric needs. It's important to reiterate that nothing will replace a medical professional's guidance, so take the following section as more of a guide than a hard rule.

How to Calculate Your Macros

While calorie counting alone is a recipe for disaster, macro counting is how you're going to manage the diet and see the best results. In the previous section, you read that without knowing the specifics of your body, understanding your needs would be difficult. That shouldn't discourage you from trying or seeking a general rule to start with.

The best way to start to calculate macros is to know your Basal Metabolic Rate, or BMR. This is the amount of energy expended while at rest in a neutrally temperate environment and when your digestive system has had no new food for 12 hours. Several formulas can calculate your BMR, but the one this book will use is the Revised Harris-Benedict Equation, which is as follows:

For men:

BMR = 13.397W + 4.799H - 5.677A + 88.362

For women:

BMR = 9.247W + 3.098H - 4.330A + 4471/293

W is body weight in kg

H is body height in cm

A is age

After knowing your BMR, you can move on to the next step. You need to increase your caloric intake by five to fifteen percent of the BMR if your goal is to gain weight or reduce it by 15-25 percent if your goal is to lose weight.

Naturally, your caloric intake needs will increase if you're physically active. The best way to calculate your physical activity is with the following formulas:

Sedentary = BMR x 1.2 (little or no exercise, desk job)

Lightly active = BMR x 1.375 (light exercise/ sports 1-3 days/week)

Moderately active = BMR x 11/25 (moderate exercise/ sports 6-7 days/week)

Very active = BMR x 1.725 (hard exercise every day, or exercising 2 xs/day)

Extra active = BMR x 1.9 (hard exercise 2 or more times per day, or training for marathon, or triathlon, etc.

Finally, you can calculate where your total macros are going to come from in your food using this as reference:

Protein intake should be between 0.7–1.0 grams per lb. of body weight.

Fat intake should be between 1/4–0.4 grams per lb. of body weight.

All remaining calories are allotted for carbohydrates.

The section of the book with the two two-week programs will feature a template to help you plan your own diet. You can choose from any of the recipes in this book to build the perfect diet based on your preference and your favorite flavors. You can customize your diet to help you get more protein, less calories, or incorporate healthy fats. The importance of you making your own diet is so you can not only be conscious of what you are eating, but it will also help you take control of your health. Following a macro diet can help you achieve the kind of health results you are striving for, whatever they may be.

The goal is to reach an ideal balance with your macros according to what your macros demand. With the formulas taken above, it's simple to create your own two-week program based on your own needs. Of course, it's always best to consult a doctor before pursuing this diet to account for any pre-existing conditions and to consider your own goals for this diet.

Regardless, with the formulas in hand, you'll be able to reach the goals you're looking for. You can apply your own measurements if you'd like to calculate your own macros when using this book.

How to Use this Cookbook

So now you know what the Macro diet is and how to calculate your macros. How does this book help you? This cookbook is filled with delicious Macro diet recipes, and all of them can help you pursue this diet and your health goals. That said, the primary key of this diet isn't the food. It's the balance of what you eat and what you do. You can't just eat solely from the dessert or snack chapters and expect to see results. Likewise, you can't eat only pizza and pasta dishes without any significant protein for your health. The best way is to balance the four groups throughout the day since it's not always possible to balance the groups at every meal. So, let's say you eat a meal where beef was the main focus for lunch, and you have a vegetable-focused dinner. That's an example of the balance that you should strive for. To make things simpler, every recipe will be marked as either protein or carbohydrate-focused to give you a general idea of what you're eating. There will be recipes with both listed, and those dishes give the best balance. Also, you should remember that you must exercise if you want to see meaningful results, as the macro diet is part of a healthier lifestyle that you're pursuing. It's only one of the two factors necessary for physical health.

To close this introduction, it's best to understand that failure is a possibility when pursuing this diet just like any other. Will you make mistakes and choose to eat something not healthy for you? Possibly. Will you go out with your friends and your family and select something sub-optimal for your health? That's a given. Will you want to forget about this entire diet and go back to your poor eating habits? Sure. What's important, however, is not giving up on yourself or on the diet. If you have one meal that's not on the diet or go one day without eating the diet, then that's fine, and you shouldn't think less of yourself or the diet for it. The one thing that's not acceptable is giving up. If you're serious about making a change in your life and your health, then it's not something you can give up on. Why would you want to, considering no one else will take care of you but you? As long as you keep yourself on the right path and get past the bumps in the road, you will reach your goals.

Chapter 1: Understanding the Main Four Food Groups of this Diet

Balance and Why it is Key

Balance, balance, balance. It's what everyone talks about, but no one understands it. Some people believe it means having balanced meals. Others believe it means balancing exercise and a diet. Others think it means following a food pyramid and its guidelines. The only one that's correct is the balanced meals, but that doesn't mean every meal you eat has to balance the following four main aspects you'll read about in this chapter. It just means you have to balance all four of those aspects throughout the day.

At the end of the book, you will create a two-week diet program so you can try out this diet for yourself. You'll find that many of the meals prescribed don't balance the four attributes in an ideal sense. The meals add up a sufficient portion of all four attributes in a single day, which is the best way to fuel the body.

It's also important to note that each of the four attributes plays a different role in your body. In the introduction, you read that your body is a complex machine. Like any complex machine, fuel alone isn't enough to make it run, and proper maintenance is vital to ensure it works properly. The Macro diet does both by introducing the foods your body needs for fuel while maintaining it internally.

Now you will read more about macros incorporated into your diet and the emphasis on vegetables. This will help you understand more about how they work in the body and why you should be open to eating them all within the parameters of the macro diet.

Carbohydrates, Evil or Misunderstood?

Carbohydrates have a bad reputation in the diet world. Every diet out their advocates for low carbohydrates, or no carbohydrates at all. What did carbohydrates do to earn this reputation, and how should you approach them in your diet?

First, it should be noted that carbohydrates aid in your body's energy production. Fitness coaches will advocate eating carbohydrates on days you do strength training to give your body the energy it needs and to follow the regimen you want. If you've ever heard someone say "I need to work this off" after a big meal, they should be referring to a meal with carbohydrates in them. If you don't exercise after eating carbohydrates, then your body stores the excess energy and causes you to gain weight. But why does this happen?

Carbohydrates, like any other food that enters your body, go through a process as they travel through your digestive system, and as they are broken down within your body, they're reduced to a final form that gets passed along to the rest of your body. The final form of carbohydrates is glucose, which is sugar. Sugar comes in different forms, too, but the one from carbohydrates is processed differently from sweet foods and is converted to energy to support physical activity.

Of course, you might be thinking how you're going to get your balance of carbohydrates without exercising every day, as that's not feasible for most people given their schedules and other aspects of their lives. That's where fast and slow carbohydrates come in. The difference between fast and slow carbohydrates is how fast it takes your body to break down the food to make sugar. Fast carbohydrates turn into sugar faster because they're easier for your body to break down into sugars, whereas slow carbohydrates have more than just carbohydrates and other nutritional value, making them more beneficial.

Fast carbohydrates are the ones you should watch out for and eat sparingly. These are white bread, potatoes, refined grains, and most pastas. Pasta and pizza also have fast carbohydrates depending on what they're made with, so it's best to be knowledgeable about what kind of fast carbohydrates you're consuming. Of course, if you're planning on exercising on the days you eat fast carbohydrates, then you're good to go. Otherwise, your intake should be the slow carbohydrates.

Slow carbohydrates are the carbohydrates you'll eat when you're not exercising that day. Examples of slow carbohydrates include nuts, whole grains, fruits, vegetables, legumes, and oats. While vegetables are in their own category, it is important to note that they're here because it proves that not all carbohydrates are bad for you. Which leads back to the main point of balance. Slow carbohydrates will appear in most recipes in this book and as replacements for fast carbohydrates where it's applicable, which will continue to keep the balance you'll strive to maintain.

A Note on Gluten

Gluten is an aspect of many fast carbohydrates. It doesn't affect how carbohydrates enter the body in any meaningful way. That said, people with Celiac Disease cannot properly break down gluten, leading to complications in regularity. If you do not have Celiac Disease, gluten won't matter when eating fast carbohydrates.

Protein, Your Best Friend

Protein is the focus of your health and food intake. Protein is what keeps your muscles and bones strong and gives your body endurance for physical activity. Almost every recipe in this cookbook will include protein because it is vital to the well-being of your body. Of course, as with carbohydrates, not all proteins are made equal. Cheese and milk are both protein sources, but they're not as healthy as lean meats or vegetables and legumes with protein in them. Proteins will be the focus of most of the dishes in this cookbook. Proteins are not only good for you, but they fill you up. Carbohydrates, fats, and vegetables also all play essential roles in your nutrition. Still, protein will be the focus for your muscles.

Dietary Restrictions? No Problem!

Of course, it's important to note that proteins are among the most controversial food groups for people who have dietary restrictions. Proteins are separated into different chapters for the different types of meal restrictions available. This book is applicable to everyone who reads it regardless of dietary restrictions. If you can't or won't eat certain animal products for moral, health, or religious reasons, you can still pursue the macro diet. You can do so by looking at the sections of protein you're interested in and ignoring those you won't eat.

While most known proteins are animal meats or animal products, that does not mean vegans and vegetarians can't get their protein intake. Soy protein and other plant-based replacement proteins will be a focus here. Of course, that's not to say that you have to eat tofu or soy protein products to get your intake. Several recipes within this cookbook will make sure you get your protein intake. The vegetarian and vegan chapter will ensure that protein will be a part of almost every meal you eat while on this diet. Even if you're not a vegetarian, it never hurts to try a vegetable dish for a nice change of pace. You'll still get the required protein you need for success on the macro diet.

A Note on Dairy

Dairy products such as milk, cheese, and yogurt will be a part of this book. It's important to note that these foods will be used sparingly or as part of dessert options. There are great alternatives to cow's milk, such as goat's milk, which is easier on the stomach, or milk from nuts and seeds, such as soy and almond milk. These are healthy alternatives to standard cow's milk for health reasons, provided that their sugar count remains low. The same applies to cheese and yogurt, where vegan and vegetarian options exist for both of these great food items.

Fats, Not Free

Fats used to have a bad reputation, and to this day, many people believe fats are bad for your health. Fat-free foods were common in the '80s and '90s because the general belief was that fats make you unhealthy. What followed was the sharpest rise in health complications the modern world had ever seen because fats weren't the cause of health issues. The same food that gave carbohydrates their bad reputation was the problem: sugar. Most fat-free foods lacked flavor which was replaced by adding refined sugar, causing all the health problems we are trying to fix today. Of course, that doesn't mean all fats are good, just as not all carbohydrates are bad. It's essential to know the difference between the different kinds of fats and what you're eating.

What are fats, and what role do they play in nutrition? Fats are among the three essential nutrients your body needs to function, with carbohydrates and protein being the others. Fats are separated into different categories based on how they're processed before being introduced to the body. There are three kinds of fats, each of them having various benefits and detriments for your body and understanding them and their role will help you with your health goals.

The three types of fat are saturated fats, unsaturated fats, and trans fats. Of these three, unsaturated fats are the best for you, as they can lower LDL or 'bad' cholesterol levels and are prevalent in healthy foods. Unsaturated fats are separated into two different categories, as well. These are monounsaturated fats and polyunsaturated fats. Monounsaturated fats come from peanut, olive, and canola oils (canola oil can also be a good source of polyunsaturated fats), avocados, certain nuts, and seeds. Polyunsaturated fats come from Sunflower, corn, soybean, and flaxseed oils, walnuts, flax seeds, and fish. The Omega-3 prevalent in fish is an essential unsaturated fat that your body cannot create. There's less to balance out with unsaturated fats due to their health benefits.

Saturated fats are where things may get confusing. These are the fats associated with most animal protein sources and dairy and can be fattening independently. When previous wisdom claimed that fats were bad for you, saturated fats and trans fats were the main focus. That said, they still can be fattening and raise harmful cholesterol levels. This is why balance in the food you eat and the exercise you do is essential. Yes, it's critical to get protein, but eating a cheeseburger on its own with no exercise or regard to balance is a recipe for disaster. Saturated fats are the unfortunate by-product of animal protein and dairy. Still, the protein benefit outweighs the detriments if it's appropriately managed alongside the rest of your diet and your exercise regimen. Most recipes in this book will limit the sources of saturated fats to avoid health complications. Where it's applicable, they'll be replaced with unsaturated fats.

Trans fats are the worst when it comes to fats. These are made by heating liquid vegetable oils in hydrogen gas and a catalyst, creating a process called hydrogenation. This process is used by the fast food and restaurant industries. To make matters worse, hydrogenated oils can be used repeatedly, further increasing trans fats. Any benefit of canola oil or olive oil, usually unsaturated fats, is gone when they turn into trans fats. Restaurants that offer fried foods can cook hundreds of meals using the same oil before changing it, thus increasing the risk of trans fats. Trans fats are also prevalent in recipes that use hydrogenated oils, such as cakes and cookies, so it's not just fried foods you should watch out for. Not only do trans fats raise your harmful cholesterol levels, but they can also damage blood vessels, lower good cholesterol levels, and increase your risk of cancer. There is no balancing out trans fats in any meaningful way. It's best for your long-term health to avoid them altogether or enjoy foods that have them sparingly.

Vegetables and Micronutrients

Vegetables also get a bad rap, but for an entirely different reason than carbohydrates and fats. Many people refuse to eat them because they are often not palatable or filling, choosing to opt for diets with higher protein or carbohydrate proportions. The reason for this is simple. Most people grew up with parents or loved ones who didn't know how to prepare vegetables other than steaming them or boiling them. It's a sad reality, but the best way to overcome this is to think about how you would prepare meat and compare that to how you would prepare vegetables. Would you steam a steak or boil a chicken? Of course not. The flavor of those foods would be diminished and eating them would be a miserable affair. Now consider eating grilled corn on the cob. Doesn't the smell of the corn entice you? Doesn't the bite into a warm cob followed by an explosion of the sweet flavor in the juices sound exhilarating? That's what you need to think about when it comes to vegetables. They are versatile too, considering how many of them there are and the different ways they can all be incorporated into delicious meals. Some of the best pizza and pasta sauces are made with vegetables. Many vegetables can be prepared in different ways while still being the vegetable you set out to eat. You can grill some vegetables with salt and pepper like a steak and get delicious results, too. There's no limit to their flavor and complexity if you're willing to explore and try new things.

Micronutrients vs. Macronutrients

Vegetables are covered in their own section of this chapter because they are home to micronutrients, the essential vitamins and minerals your body needs to function. While other foods with macronutrients have micronutrients, vegetables will always have more when you eat them. The good thing about micronutrients is that you don't need them as much as you need macronutrients for your body to function. That's not to say they should be avoided altogether, nor will they be in the course of the diet, but they will take the back seat for this particular diet because the goal here is to manage your macronutrients rather than your micronutrients.

That said, if you suffer from any deficiencies regarding your micronutrients, then it's best to look for more detailed information regarding the foods you eat to ensure that you make up for them. Otherwise, Macronutrients will be the star of the recipes you'll read, and managing these will help your body reach its ideal and healthy shape.

Chapter 2: Soups

The Mighty Soup

Soups are a misunderstood food for many. Most people grew up eating canned soups or simple broths made by loved ones to help through cold climates or illnesses. The side effect was little thought given to their nutritional value or complexity. As a result, soups are seen as either an appetizer or a quick meal. In truth, soups are among the most potent foods you can eat for your health and the flavors you consume. Not only are soups among the best ways to mix all four food groups in one meal, but they're also perfect for busy people who don't have the time to cook meals earlier in the day. Soups are also easy on the digestive system. They are absorbed faster by your body because they don't have many solids in them, or the solids present in soups are softer due to their exposure to the broth. Note the word 'broth' is used to denote the liquid part of the soups because broths are the lifeblood of many soup recipes, and the flavor in the broth will permeate all the other ingredients. Hot water as the broth is a bad idea, and it will make you hate soups. That's not to say water won't be used to make the broth, but the water itself is not a broth you should focus on, which is the unfortunate truth of how many people see soups.

The soups in this cookbook are separated into three categories of hot, cold, and vegetarian. The hot recipes are perfect for winter months or people living in cold environments. The cold recipes are perfect for the summer months and people living in warmer climates. The vegetarian soups will fall under both categories while limiting or excluding animal products altogether. The mighty soups are awaiting you. Give them a try and see their effectiveness.

Shopping List

Recommended Appliances

- Soup pot (roughly one gallon in size will do)
- Vegetable grater
- High-powered blender or food processor
- Large saucepan
- Pressure Cooker

Recommended Ingredients

- Chicken Stock
- Vegetable Stock
- Onions
- Garlic cloves
- Chicken fillets
- Scallions
- Olive oil
- Carrots
- Tomatoes
- Greek Yogurt
- Oregano, thyme, dill, and other preferred spices, fresh or dried.
- Canned beans
- Canned corn
- Salt and pepper

Hot Soups

Stuffed Pepper Soup (Protein)

Servings: 8 servings　　　　　　　　　　　　　　　　　　　　　**Serving size: 28 oz. of soup**

Ingredients
- 2 lb. lean ground beef
- 3 bell peppers
- 1 tbsp. minced garlic
- 1 medium-sized onion
- 1 head of cauliflower, or 2 bags of frozen riced cauliflower
- 2 beef bouillon cubes
- 1½ tbsps. Italian seasoning
- 1 small can of tomato paste
- 1 can of diced tomatoes
- 1 tbsp. olive oil
- 3 cups of water or vegetarian broth
- Salt and pepper for taste

Directions Preheat soup pot to medium heat.
Chop bell peppers to desired shape. Dice onions to desired shape.
Add olive oil to the pot once hot. Cook ground beef until brown with garlic, onion, and peppers.
Drain any grease. Add all other ingredients except the cauliflower, stirring occasionally (skip steps 5-7 if using frozen riced cauliflower).
Prep cauliflower by removing leaves and stems. Chop cauliflower into large pieces and place in a blender or food processor.
Process cauliflower on Pulse until it achieves a rice shape. Add riced cauliflower to the pot.
Allow soup to simmer until cauliflower is fully cooked.
Serve in bowls and enjoy!

Nutritional Information per serving Calories: 246 Fat: 8g Protein: 27g

Instant Pot Cabbage Soup (Protein)

Servings: 8 servings　　　　　　　　　　　　　　　　　　　　　**Serving size: 1 ½ cups of soup**

Ingredients
- 5 cups chopped green cabbage
- 4 cups beef stock
- 1 lb. ground beef
- 28-oz. can diced tomatoes
- 1 cup riced cauliflower (frozen or fresh)
- ½ cup diced onions
- ½ cup diced carrots
- 1 tbsp. olive oil
- 1 ½ tsps. table salt
- 1 tsp. dried oregano
- 1 tsp. dried thyme

Directions Preheat pressure cooker to medium heat on sauté mode (Skip steps 2-4 if using frozen cauliflower).
Prep cauliflower by removing leaves and stems. Chop cauliflower into large pieces and place in a blender or food processor. Process on Pulse the cauliflower until it achieves a rice shape.
Dice onions and carrots to desired size.
When the pressure cooker display says 'hot' spread olive oil across the pan. Add beef, onions and carrots to the pressure cooker. Stir frequently until vegetables are soft. Turn off sauté mode.
Add all other ingredients into the pressure cooker. Secure and seal the pressure cooker's lid.
Cook for 20 minutes at high pressure.
Allow 15 minutes for natural release, then manually release any more pressure with the knob.
Uncover the lid, serve into bowls, and enjoy!

Nutritional Information per serving Calories: 160 Fat: 7 g Carbohydrates: 8 g Protein: 13 g

Skinless Chicken Ramen (Carbohydrates)

Servings: 4 servings

Serving size: 21/4 oz. noodles, 1 egg, 2 oz. chicken, ¼ cup carrots, ¼ cup cabbage, ¼ cup bean sprouts, 1 ¼ cups broth, ½ scallion

Ingredients
- 8 oz. whole wheat, gluten-free ramen noodles, soba noodles or whole wheat spaghetti
- 4 eggs
- 3 cups reduced-sodium chicken, pork or vegetable broth
- 1 ½ tsps. reduced-sodium soy sauce
- 1 10-oz. boneless, skinless chicken breast
- 1 cup cabbage
- 1 cup carrot
- 2 scallions
- 1 cup bean sprouts

Directions Boil 2 cups of water in a saucepan.
Chop chicken, carrots, scallions, and cabbage to desired shapes.
Prepare a large bowl filled with ice water.
Place bean sprouts in boiling water for one minute.
Remove bean sprouts from boiling water and place in ice water. Remove them when they're chilled.
Dump the boiled water and turn off the heat.
Place the eggs in the saucepan with water going one inch over the top of the shells.
Prepare another saucepan with two cups of water, the chosen broth and soy sauce and bring to a boil.
Prepare another bowl with ice water.
Put the eggs over high heat until the water boils. Put the boiled eggs in a separate ice water bowl for seven minutes.
When the other saucepan boils, add the chicken and reduce heat to a simmer.
Add the carrots and cabbage to the broth bowl, stirring throughout until the chicken is fully cooked.
Using the same boiling bowl for the eggs, cook the noodles to desired consistency or according to package requirements.
Put the noodles in different bowls according to the serving size.
Halve eggs, remove the shells, and divide them and the bean sprouts across the bowls according to the serving size.
Pour broth into bowls and garnish with scallions.
Serve and enjoy!

Nutritional Information per serving Calories: 160 Fat: 8 g Carbohydrates: 47 g Protein: 35 g

Chicken Posole (Protein)

Servings: 4

Serving size: 28 oz. of soup.

Ingredients
- 1 lb. of chicken breast
- 4 cups chicken stock
- 1 bay leaf
- ½ tsp. fresh thyme
- ½ tsp. fresh oregano
- 1 tbsp. olive oil
- 2 cloves of garlic
- 1 tsp. cumin
- 1 tsp. salt
- ¾ tsp. chili powder
- ½ tsp. coriander
- ¼ tsp. red pepper flakes
- 1 cup canned hominy

Directions Drain the hominy from the can and put it into a bowl with water. Let it sit for one day.
Preheat the sauce pan to medium heat.
Chop the thyme and oregano into fine pieces. Crush the garlic cloves.
Chop the chicken into slices for consistent shapes, seasoning with salt and pepper.
Add olive oil to the pan. Add the chicken to the pan, browning both sides.
Lower heat, then cover the pan and cook the chicken for 12 more minutes, flipping once more at the six-minute mark. Take off heat when ready.
While the chicken is cooking, prepare a soup pot at medium heat. Add the stock to the soup pot and bring to a simmer.
Add all ingredients except the chicken and hominy to the soup pot, simmer for 15 minutes stirring occasionally.

As the soup simmers, shred the chicken using two forks.
Drain the water from the hominy and add it with the chicken to the soup. Warm the soup to medium to cook everything through.
Discard the bay leaf, serve into bowls, and enjoy!

Nutritional Information per serving Calories: 238 Fat: 4.7 g Carbohydrates: 8.2 g Protein: 39.3 g

Roasted Chicken Soup (Protein)

Servings: 4 **Serving size: 28 oz. of soup.**

Ingredients
- Half a rotisserie/roasted chicken
- 1 tbsp. extra virgin olive oil
- 2 cups low-sodium chicken broth
- 3 cups low-sodium vegetable broth
- ½ cup onion
- ½ cup celery
- ½ cup carrot
- 1 tsp. kosher salt
- 1 cup cooked brown rice
- ¼ cup chopped fresh herbs of your choice.

Directions Preheat a soup pot to medium heat.
Dice the herbs, celery, onions, and carrot.
Remove the skin from the chicken.
Take both white and dark meat and shred. Save the other half of the chicken for later or other uses.
Add olive oil to the pot. Add celery, onion, and carrot to the soup pot and cook until soft.
Add both broths and salt to the pot, bring it to a boil, lowering to a simmer once boiling. Simmer for ten minutes.
Add the chicken, rice, and herbs. Simmer for five minutes.
Serve into separate bowls and enjoy!

Nutritional Information per serving Calories: 372 Fat: 9.9 g Carbohydrates: 42.1/2 g Protein: 25.6 g

White Bean and Kale Soup (Carbohydrates)

Servings: 6 **Serving size: 28 oz. of soup.**

Ingredients
- 1 tbsp. extra virgin olive oil
- 8 large garlic cloves
- 1 medium yellow onion
- 6 cups chopped raw kale
- 4 cups low-sodium vegetable broth
- 30 oz. white beans, such as cannellini or navy, rinsed and drained
- 4 Roma tomatoes
- 1 tsp. dried oregano
- 1 tsp. dried basil
- ½ tsp. salt
- ¼ tsp. pepper
- ¼ tsp. crushed red pepper
- 6 tbsps. of freshly shredded Parmesan

Directions Drain the water from the canned beans and put them in a bowl with water. Let them sit for one day.
Preheat soup pot over medium heat.
Chop the onions, tomatoes, garlic, and kale.
Add garlic and onions to the pot. Sauté until soft. Add the kale and sauté until the kale is soft and wilted.
Add all other ingredients except for parmesan cheese. Lower heat and simmer for five minutes.
Transfer to a blender and puree until smooth. Return mixture to pot and simmer for 15 minutes.
Serve in bowls, sprinkle 1 tbsp. of Parmesan cheese per serving, and enjoy!

Nutritional Information per serving Calories: 300 Fat: 4.6 g Carbohydrates: 49.7 g Protein: 17.1 g

Chicken and Lentil Soup (Carbohydrates)

Servings: 6   **Serving size: Two cups**

Ingredients
- 2 lbs. chicken breasts boneless & skinless
- 1 ½ cups dry green or brown lentils
- 8 cups chicken stock low sodium
- 14 oz. can coconut milk light or full fat
- 2 tsps. garlic powder
- 1 ¼ tsps. salt
- 3 cups canned corn
- 3 handfuls of spinach or preferred greens
- ⅓ cup cilantro
- 3 scallions
- Tortilla chips for garnish

Directions Put the lentils in a bowl with water. Let them sit for one day.
Preheat soup pot to medium heat.
Chop chicken into thin pieces for soup.
Finely chop cilantro and scallions.
Pour broth and coconut water into the soup pot. Immediately add the chicken, garlic powder, and salt. Bring it to a boil.
Add the lentils and lower heat to a simmer. Cover the soup and stir occasionally for 45 minutes.
Strain the corn to remove the liquid from the can.
Add the spinach, corn, scallions and cilantro to the soup. Stir well to mix the ingredients.
Serve in bowls and enjoy!

Nutritional Information per serving Calories: 555 Fat: 28 g Carbohydrates: 49 g Protein: 17.1 g

Pork Ramen with Zucchini Noodles (Protein)

Servings: 5   **Serving size: 28 oz. of soup.**

Ingredients
- 1 lb. ground pork
- 6 cups beef broth
- 4 scallions
- 4 cloves garlic
- 1 tbsp. ginger
- 3 cups kale
- 2 tbsps. olive oil
- ¼ low sodium soy sauce
- 1 tbsp. apple cider vinegar
- 1 tbsp. fish sauce
- 1 large zucchini

Directions Preheat soup pot to medium heat.
Chop the scallions, garlic, and kale into desired shape for soup. Spiralize the zucchini into noodle shapes. Grate the ginger.
Spread olive oil in the soup pot. Place the pork in the pot and cook until almost brown.
Add the scallions, garlic, and ginger and mix with the pork.
Add all other ingredients except the zucchini noodles to the soup pot and bring to a low boil.
Lower heat to a simmer and add Zucchini noodles. Cook and stir until tender.

Nutritional Information per serving Calories: 311 Fat: 20 g Carbohydrates: 9 g Protein: 21 g

Powerful Chicken Noodle Soup (Protein)

Servings: 6   **Serving size: 28 oz. of soup.**

Ingredients
- ½ tbsp. olive oil
- 6 oz. cooked chicken
- 7 cups chicken stock
- ½ cup onion
- 3 stalks of celery
- 2 cups of carrots
- 2 cloves of fresh garlic
- 2 bay leaves
- ½ tbsp. fresh or dried parsley
- 6 oz. uncooked egg noodle pasta
- Salt and pepper to taste

Directions Preheat the soup pot to medium heat.
Chop the onions, parsley, and celery into small pieces for soup.
Cut the cooked chicken into desired size for soup.

Drizzle olive oil into the pan. Add all chopped ingredients and bay leaves into the pan.
When they sizzle, reduce heat to low and stir. Cook for five more minutes.
Add the garlic and stir for another minute. Add the broth and bring to a boil.
Cook the pasta until noodles are soft. Add the chicken when two minutes are left for noodle consistency.
Serve into bowls and enjoy!

Nutritional Information per serving Calories: 243 Fat: 5 g Carbohydrates: 35 g Protein: 11 g

Fish and Vegetable Soup (Protein)

Servings: 4 **Serving size: 28 oz. of soup.**

Ingredients
- 1 lb. firm fresh white fish fillets of any white fish of your choice
- 1 tbsp. butter
- ¼ cup chopped onion
- 1 clove of garlic
- 3 ½ cups chicken broth
- 1 cup carrots
- 1 cup frozen cut green beans
- ½ cup frozen corn
- ½ tsp. salt
- ½ tsp. dried basil leaves
- ¼ tsp. dried oregano leaves
- ⅛ tsp. pepper

Directions Preheat soup pot to medium heat.
Thinly chop carrots, onions, and garlic.
Melt butter in the soup pot and add onions and garlic. Stir until garlic is brown.
Add every other ingredient except fish and bring to a boil, stirring throughout.
Lower heat to a simmer and cook for eight minutes.
Add fish and cook uncovered for another seven minutes until fish flakes, stirring occasionally.
Serve into bowls and enjoy!

Nutritional Information per serving Calories: 190 Fat: 4.5 g Carbohydrates: 11 g Protein: 25 g

Macro Chowder (Carbohydrates)

Servings: 5 **Serving size: Two cups of soup.**

Ingredients
- 1 tbsp. avocado oil or organic canola oil
- 1 large onion
- 1 cup celery
- 1 tbsp. chopped garlic
- ¾ tsp. dry thyme or 1 ½ tsps. fresh
- ½ tsp. salt or to taste
- ¼ tsp. ground white pepper
- ¼ tsp. fennel seeds
- A pinch of nutmeg
- ½ cup dry white wine
- 2 cups lower sodium bottled clam juice
- 2 ½ cups lower sodium chicken broth
- 4 medium red potatoes
- 2 tbsps. of all-purpose flour
- 1 lb. raw shucked clams
- 8 oz. Alaskan cod or Sablefish
- ½ cup half-and-half cream
- Parsley or chives for garnish

Directions Preheat the soup pan to medium heat.
Chop the potatoes into quarters. Finely chop the celery, thyme (if using fresh), garlic, and onions.
Cut the fish into appropriate chunks for soup.
Add the oil, onion, celery, garlic, thyme, fennel, salt, pepper, and nutmeg. Stir until the onions begin to brown.
Add the wine over high heat, stirring until wine almost entirely evaporates.
Add clam juice, potatoes, and chicken broth. Cover and bring soup to a simmer, stirring occasionally.
Reduce heat to medium-low and stir for ten minutes or until potatoes are soft.
Add in the flour and whisk until the soup achieves thickness.
Add in clams and fish and stir until the fish is fully opaque.
Serve into bowls and garnish with parsley or chives as desired and enjoy!

Nutritional Information per serving Calories: 349 Fat: 7 g Carbohydrates: 41 g Protein: 25 g

Macro Pho (Carbohydrates)

Servings: 2 **Serving size: 28 oz. of soup.**

Ingredients
- 1 section of ginger, ¾ oz.
- 2 scallions
- 1 small bunch cilantro sprigs
- 1 ½ tsps. coriander seeds
- 1 whole clove
- 3 ½ cups unsalted chicken stock
- 2 cups of water
- 1 skinless, boneless chicken breast
- 3 oz. dried flat rice noodles
- 1 tsp. fish sauce
- Fresh basil leaves, mint leaves, mung bean sprouts, sliced red Fresno chili, and lime wedges, for garnish

Directions Preheat the soup pot to medium heat.
Cut the ginger and scallions into small slices.
Chop the leaves of the cilantro coarsely, keeping the stems aside for now.
Toast coriander seeds in the soup pot for two minutes until fragrant.
Add the green onions ginger for 30 seconds, stirring throughout.
Take the pot off heat and cool for 15 seconds. Pour in soup stock and return the pot to the heat.
Add the water, cilantro stems, and chicken. Bring the pot to a boil and then lower the heat to a simmer for 30 minutes, stirring throughout until the chicken is fully opaque.
While broth is simmering, soak the rice noodles in a bowl of hot water.
Drain the noodles and rinse them, setting them aside for now.
After simmering for ten minutes, remove the chicken from the pot and flush with cold water.
Drain the chicken and cut it into bite-size pieces for soup.
Strain the broth, removing all solids from the pot and discarding them.
Add fish sauce and return to heat. Bring to a boil.
Place the noodles in noodle strainers according to servings and cook for one minute.
Divide the broth and noodles into two servings in bowls and serve, garnishing as desired. Enjoy!

Nutritional Information per serving Calories: 360 Fat: 3.1 g Carbohydrates: 47 g Protein: 35 g

Cold Soups

Potato Zucchini Vichyssoise (Carbohydrates)

Servings: 2 servings **Serving size: 28 oz. of soup**

Ingredients
- 2 medium potatoes
- 1 cup sliced zucchini
- ½ cup canned white beans
- 1 cup 2% milk
- 1 cup chicken broth
- ¼ avocado
- 2 tbsps. chopped parsley
- ¼ tsp. sea salt
- 1 squash blossoms
- Black pepper to taste

Directions Place beans in a bowl with water, submerging all the beans. Let sit for one day.
Boil water in a large pot.
Chop potatoes, zucchini, avocado, parsley, and squash blossoms.
Add potatoes to bowl and lower heat to a simmer. Add zucchini to the bowl and cook until potatoes and zucchini are tender. Remove potatoes and zucchini from the bowl and let them sit until chilled.
Drain the beans and mix every ingredient except the squash blossoms in a blender and puree until smooth.
Chill for 45 minutes.
Serve in two separate bowls and garnish with the squash blossoms and black pepper. Enjoy!

Nutritional Information per serving Calories: 457 Fat: 8.9 g Carbohydrates: 74.7 g Protein: 23.1 g

Chilled Avocado Soup (Carbohydrates)

Servings: 4 servings　　　　　　　　　　**Serving size:** 28 oz. of total soup

Ingredients
- 2 avocados
- ½ cup full fat dairy free yogurt
- ¼ cup lime juice
- ¼ cup cilantro fresh
- 1 Cucumber
- Salt and pepper for garnish
- Water as needed for thinning

Directions Seed and skin the cucumber, cutting it into small pieces.
Cut the avocados into small pieces. Finely chop the cilantro.
Add all ingredients to a blender and puree until smooth. Add water as needed to reach desired consistency.
Serve and enjoy!

Nutritional Information per serving Calories: 281 Fat: 24.1/2 g Carbohydrates: 14 g Protein: 5 g

Chilled Almond Soup (Carbohydrates)

Servings: 4 servings　　　　　　　　　　**Serving size:** 28 oz. of soup

Ingredients
- 1 cup blanched Marcona almonds
- 2 slices of white bread
- 1 small clove of garlic
- 1-2 tsps. of sherry vinegar to adjust for taste
- 1 apple
- Salt to taste
- 1 cup of cold water
- ¼ cup of extra virgin olive oil

Directions Leave the bread slices out overnight.
Place the almonds in a bowl of water overnight.
Drain the water from the almonds and cut the bread into cubes.
Core and cut the apple into cubes. Slice the garlic cloves into small pieces.
Add all ingredients except salt and vinegar to a blender and puree.
Add the salt and vinegar to taste.
Chill in the refrigerator, serve into bowls when chilled, and enjoy!

Nutritional Information per serving Calories: 383.4 Fat: 31.65 g Carbohydrates: 20.41 g Protein: 8.89 g

Cheese and Pineapple Soup (Carbohydrates)

Servings: 4 servings　　　　　　　　　　**Serving size:** 28 oz. of soup

Ingredients
- 3 cups pineapple
- 1 tbsp. lime juice
- 3 tbsps. guava juice
- 1 tbsp. lemon juice
- 3 dates
- 1 tbsp. fresh basil
- ½ cup coconut cream
- ¼ cup banana
- 1 tbsp. cotija cheese

Directions Remove the pits from the dates.
Core the pineapple and cut it into chunks for blending.
Put all ingredients into the blender except for the cheese and puree until smooth.
Chill in the refrigerator. Serve in bowls when chilled and garnish with the cheese. Enjoy!

Nutritional Information per serving Calories: 246 Fat: 7 g Carbohydrates: 48 g Protein: 2 g

Chilled Avocado Bacon Soup (Carbohydrates)

Servings: 6 servings   **Serving size:** 28 oz. of soup

Ingredients
- 2 slices of bacon
- 2 cups of low-sodium chicken broth
- 1 cup sour cream
- ¼ cup of cilantro
- 1 tbsp. lime juice
- 1 medium tomato
- 2 scallions
- ½ tsp. hot sauce

Directions Preheat a pan to high heat.
Peel and chop the avocados. Mince the cilantro. Dice the tomato.
Cook the bacon on the pan until crispy. Crumble the bacon to bits.
Mix all the ingredients except the bacon, diced tomatoes, and scallions in a blender and puree. Add salt and pepper as desired. Chill the soup until cold.
Serve into bowls and garnish with bacon, diced tomatoes, and scallions. Enjoy!

Nutritional Information per serving Calories: 229 Fat: 21 g Carbohydrates: 8 g Protein: 3 g

Cold Beet Soup (Carbohydrates)

Servings: 6 servings   **Serving size:** 28 oz. of soup

Ingredients
- 2 small beets
- 2-3 tbsps. of lemon juice
- 13.5 fl. oz. vegetable stock
- 25 oz. Greek yogurt
- 3-4 tbsps. dill
- 4 tbsps. chives
- 10 radishes
- 1 cucumber, peeled
- 1 garlic clove crushed
- 1 ½ tsps. fine sea salt

Directions Preheat the soup pot to medium heat.
Finely chop the dill and chives. Peel the beets and grate coarsely. Chop and crush the garlic clove.
Grate the cucumber coarsely.
Place greens, broth, lemon juice, and beets in the pot and bring to a boil.
Simmer for five minutes and then remove from heat. Let cool until heat is gone.
Add all remaining ingredients and stir.
Chill in the refrigerator for at least thirty minutes before serving and enjoy!

Nutritional Information per serving Calories: 229 Fat: 21 g Carbohydrates: 8 g Protein: 3 g

Chilled Cucumber Soup (Protein)

Servings: 6 servings   **Serving size:** 28 oz. of total soup

Ingredients
- 2 cups Greek yogurt
- 1 cup vegetable broth
- 2 cucumbers
- 4 scallions
- 2 tbsps. fresh dill
- 2 tbsps. fresh parsley
- 4 tsps. fresh lemon juice
- 2 tsps. salt

Directions Peel and dice the cucumbers. Chop the parsley and dill.
Puree one cucumber, parsley, and dill in a blender. Whisk the puree with the yogurt, adding in the lemon juice and salt. Add the other diced cucumber to the soup and whisk.
Chill in the refrigerator for one hour.

Nutritional Information per serving Calories: 432 Fat: 11.2 g Carbohydrates: 26.7 g Protein: 55.7 g

Chilled Asparagus Bisque (Carbohydrates)

Servings: 2 servings   **Serving size:** 28 oz. of soup

Ingredients
- 3 lbs. of asparagus
- 4 cups lower-sodium chicken broth
- 2 cups and one tbsp. of water
- 2 large leeks
- 2 tbsps. olive oil
- 2 cloves garlic
- 5 oz. baby spinach
- ½ cup heavy cream
- 1 tbsp. fresh lemon juice
- Salt and pepper to taste

Directions Preheat a soup pot to medium heat.
Rinse leeks in cold water and swish around to remove any dirt and sand.
Transfer leeks to a colander, rinsing throughout.
Dice the leeks and garlic to a small size for soup. Cut asparagus into two-inch pieces.
Add the oil, leeks, and asparagus, garlic, to the pot, stirring until garlic softens. Add the broth and salt.
Bring the pot to a boil, then lower to a simmer for 20-25 minutes.
Add spinach for the last five minutes and simmer until wilted.
Transfer soup to a blender and puree until smooth.
Refrigerate for a minimum of four hours, serve into bowls, and enjoy!

Nutritional Information per serving Calories: 461 Fat: 56.3 g Carbohydrates: 34.7 g Protein: 24.2 g

Sweet Corn Gazpacho (Carbohydrates)

Servings: 7 servings   **Serving size:** 28 oz. of soup

Ingredients
- 3 ears of Sweet Corn
- 2 cups yellow cherry tomatoes
- 1 yellow bell pepper
- ½ medium shallot
- 2-4 garlic cloves as desired
- ½ cup canned white beans
- ¾ to 1 cup vegetable stock
- ½ tsp. cayenne pepper
- 1 tsp. ground ginger
- Salt and pepper to taste

Directions Drain beans from the can and place in a bowl of water overnight.
Remove the kernels from the ears of corn. Seed and roughly chop the bell pepper.
Peel and cut the shallot into small pieces. Drain the beans and put all ingredients in a blender.
Puree until smooth and let it chill in the refrigerator for an hour or until completely chilled.

Nutritional Information per serving Calories: 97 Fat: 1 g Carbohydrates: 21 g Protein: 4 g

Spicy Pineapple Gazpacho (Carbohydrates)

Servings: 8 servings   **Serving size:** One cup of soup

Ingredients
- 1 pineapple
- 2 cucumbers
- 1 ½ cups 100% pineapple juice
- 1 jalapeno
- 2 scallions
- ½ cup cilantro
- ¼ tsp. sea salt

Directions Cut the pineapples into small chunks. Remove the seeds and stem from the jalapeno and mince it. Peel and chop the cucumbers into small chunks. Mince the cilantro. Add cucumbers and pineapples to a blender and puree until smooth. Add all other ingredients and mix until integrated. Serve in bowls and enjoy!

Nutritional Information per serving Calories: 130 Fat: 0.3 g Carbohydrates: 32.8 g Protein: 1.6 g

Vegetable Gazpacho (Carbohydrates)

Servings: 8 servings　　　　　　　　　　　　　　　　　　　　**Serving size: 28 oz. of soup**

Ingredients
- 1 can tomato or vegetable juice
- 2 cloves garlic
- 2 tbsps. lemon juice
- 2 tbsps. white wine vinegar
- 2 tbsps. Worcestershire sauce
- 2 medium tomatoes
- 1 medium red bell pepper
- 1 medium yellow bell pepper
- 1 medium green bell pepper
- 1 jalapeno pepper
- 2 stalks of celery
- 1 large cucumber
- 1 bunch of scallions
- Hot sauce, to taste
- Salt and freshly ground black pepper, to taste

Directions Place vegetable juice in the refrigerator and let chill overnight.
Mince the garlic cloves.
Finely chop the scallions, tomatoes, celery stalks, peppers, and cucumber, coring and seeding where necessary.
Add all ingredients to a large bowl and stir until fully amalgamated.
Serve and enjoy!

Nutritional Information per serving Calories: 110 Fat: 5 g Carbohydrates: 16 g Protein: 3 g

White Gazpacho with Tomato Toast (Carbohydrates)

Servings: 8 servings　　　　　　　　　　　　　　　　　　　　**Serving size: 28 oz. of total soup**

Ingredients
- 6 slices thick country white bread
- 8 slices country white bread
- 1 cucumber
- 2 cups seedless green grapes
- ½ cup blanched almonds
- 2 small cloves garlic
- 2 tsps. sherry vinegar
- ¼ cup extra virgin olive oil
- 2 tbsps. extra virgin olive oil
- 2 medium ripe tomatoes

Directions Cut the thick sliced bread into cubes.
Soak the bread cubes in water and leave aside.
Peel and seed the cucumber.
Place the almonds, garlic, grapes, and cucumber with the salt into a blender.
Pulse until chopped. Introduce the soaked bread to the blender and puree until smooth.
Add ¼ cup of olive oil and vinegar to the blender and pulse until smooth.
Put gazpacho into the refrigerator until fully chilled.
Grate the tomatoes and discard the skins.
Pulse the tomatoes to pulp in the blender with remaining olive oil and a pinch of salt.
Garnish with oil and almonds if desired.
Toast the remaining bread slices and spread the tomato mix on the toast.
Serve gazpacho in bowls and bread on separate plates and enjoy!

Nutritional Information per serving Calories: 486 Fat: 21.6 g Carbohydrates: 66 g Protein: 10.8 g

Vegetarian Soups

Roasted Tomato Basil Soup (Carbohydrates)

Servings: 4 servings

Serving size: 28 oz. of soup.

Ingredients
- 3 lbs. Roma or plum tomatoes
- 2 yellow onions
- 8 cloves Garlic
- ½ cup basil, packed leaves
- ½ tsp. oregano, dried
- 1 cups water
- 2 Salt and pepper
- 3 ½ tbsps. Olive oil

Directions Preheat oven to 400° F.
Cut the tomatoes and garlic cloves in halves.
Lay tomatoes out on a baking sheet and drizzle with olive oil. Season tomatoes and garlic cloves with salt and pepper.
Bake for 40-45 minutes. Preheat the pan to medium heat.
Dice the onions to desired shape.
Once the pan reaches medium heat, add half a tbsp. of olive oil and the onions.
Brown the onions for twenty minutes. Stir the onions every five to ten minutes until golden brown.
Once the tomatoes are done, remove them and let them rest for 10 minutes. Add tomatoes to blender or food processor and blend until smooth. Add caramelized onions and basil and blend until smooth.
Preheat the soup pot to medium-low heat. Add mixture to pot. Add water. Add oregano and salt and pepper.
Stir and allow soup to simmer for ten minutes.

Nutritional Information per serving Calories: 275 Fat: 16.2 g Carbohydrates: 35 g Protein: 5.2 g

Watermelon Gazpacho (Carbohydrates)

Servings: 6 servings

Serving size: 1 cup of soup

Ingredients
- 8 cups seedless watermelon
- 1 medium cucumber
- ½ red bell pepper
- ¼ cup fresh basil
- ¼ cup flat-leaf parsley
- 3 tbsps. red-wine vinegar
- 2 tbsps. of shallots
- 2 tbsps. extra-virgin olive oil
- ½ tsp. salt

Directions
1. Dice cucumber, watermelon, pepper, basil, parsley and shallots.
2. Add all ingredients to a blender in increments of 3 cups and puree until smooth.

Nutritional Information per serving Calories: 114 Fat: 5.1 g Carbohydrates: 17.4 g Protein: 1.8 g

Summer Corn Soup (Carbohydrates)

Servings: 4 servings

Serving size: 28 oz. of soup

Ingredients
- 4 tbsps. unsalted butter (Or two tbsps. of olive oil for vegan variation)
- 1 cup shallots
- 6 cups vegetable broth
- 6 ears of fresh corn
- ¼ tsp. kosher salt, extra to taste
- ½ tsp. freshly ground black pepper
- ½ tbsp. finely chopped fresh basil, for garnish
- 1½ tsps. finely chopped fresh thyme, for garnish

Directions Preheat the soup pot to medium low heat.
Finely chop the shallots.
Remove the kernels from all the ears of corn except for one. Cut the ears with removed kernels into halves.
Add the butter to the or olive oil to the soup pot, allowing butter to melt. Add the shallots and cook until translucent, stirring often. Add the stock, corn ear halves, corn kernels, the whole ear of corn, and salt and pepper to the soup pot.
Bring to a boil and lower heat to a simmer. Cook for ten minutes uncovered.
Remove the whole ear of corn to cool. Remove the corn ear halves.
Put the soup into a blender and puree. Introduce the soup to a new pot while straining to remove corn fibers.
Remove kernels from cooked ear and add to the soup, stirring to amalgamate.
Serve into bowls immediately for hot soup or chill for cold soup.
Garnish with basil or thyme as desired and enjoy!

Nutritional Information per serving Calories: 370 Fat: 17 g Carbohydrates: 51 g Protein: 15 g

Herbed Zucchini Soup (Protein/Carbohydrates)

Servings: 6 servings   **Serving size: 1 cup of soup**

Ingredients
- 3 cups vegetable broth
- 1½ lbs. zucchini
- 1 tbsp. of tarragon or dill
- ¾ cups of shredded reduced-fat Cheddar cheese
- ¼ tsp. salt
- ¼ tsp. freshly ground pepper

Directions Preheat saucepan to medium heat.
Chop zucchini into 1 in. slices. Chop tarragon or dill if using fresh, or prepare one tsp. of dried.
Pour broth into the pan with zucchini and herb choice. Bring to a boil over high heat.
Reduce to a simmer and cook for 7-10 minutes, or until zucchini is soft.
Puree mixture in a blender or food processor.
Return mixture to the saucepan and heat over medium low. Add cheese and stir until cheese is melted.
Serve into bowls for hot soup or refrigerate and keep up to three days for cold soup and enjoy!

Nutritional Information per serving Calories: 105 Fat: 4.1/2 g Carbohydrates: 8.9 g Protein: 8.7 g

Carrot Ginger Soup (Protein/Carbohydrates)

Servings: 4 servings   **Serving size: 28 oz. of soup**

Ingredients
- 4 tbsps. butter (or 2 tbsp. olive oil for vegan variation)
- 1½ lbs. carrots
- 1 yellow onion
- 1 tbsp. of fresh ginger
- ½ tsp. orange zest
- 4 cups chicken stock/broth or water (or vegetable stock or water for vegan variation)
- Fresh basil, green onions, or other herbs for garnish (optional)

Directions Preheat the soup pot to medium heat.
Dice the onions. Mince the ginger. Slice the carrots to bite-size medallions.
Add the butter to the pot and melt it (or simply add the olive oil) and add the onions, cooking until soft.
Add the carrots and cook for another three to five minutes. Add the ginger, orange zest, and stock and bring to a boil.
Lower heat to a simmer and cover. Let it simmer for 20 minutes.
Transfer the soup to a blender in batches and puree to desired consistency.
Serve immediately for a hot soup, or place in a refrigerator and keep up to three days and enjoy!

Nutritional Information per serving Calories: 195 Fat: 12 g Carbohydrates: 20 g Protein: 23.1 g

Spiced Carrot Soup (Carbohydrates)

Servings: 4 servings

Serving size: 28 oz. of soup

Ingredients
- 2 tbsps. coconut oil
- 3 scallions
- 1½ cloves of garlic
- 1-in. piece of ginger
- 1½ lbs. young carrots
- 1 tsp. fine sea salt
- ½ tsp. ground cinnamon
- ½ tsp. ground turmeric
- Freshly ground pepper to taste
- 4 cups (1 quart) filtered water
- ¼ cup plain dairy-free yogurt for serving
- A pinch of red pepper flakes

Directions Preheat the soup pan to medium heat.
Chop scallions into thin slices for soup. Chop carrots to bite-size medallions. Thinly slice the ginger root.
Add coconut oil soup pan and let it melt.
Add the scallions and ginger slices and cook for one minute, being careful not to let them brown.
Add carrots, salt, cinnamon, and turmeric, and cook for another one to two minutes, stirring occasionally.
Add water and bring the soup to a boil. Lower heat to a simmer and cook for 25 minutes until carrots are soft.
Puree mixture in a blender.
Let it sit in the refrigerator for three hours if serving cold, otherwise, pour into bowls and enjoy!

Nutritional Information per serving Calories: 132 Fat: 7 g Carbohydrates: 17 g Protein: 2 g

Pea and Mint Soup (Carbohydrates)

Servings: 4 servings

Serving size: 28 oz. of soup

Ingredients
- ½ tbsp. butter or one tbsp. of olive oil for vegan variation
- 1 large shallot
- 2 cups chicken stock or vegetable stock for vegan variation
- 10 fresh mint leaves
- 1 lb. frozen baby peas
- Salt and freshly ground pepper to taste

Directions Preheat the soup pan to medium-high heat.
Peel and mince shallot. Allow butter to melt in the pot or add olive oil. Add minced shallot and cook for one minute.
Add the stock and the mint leaves, bringing the soup to a boil. Add the frozen peas and let the soup reach a boil again.
Lower heat to a simmer and cook for four minutes or until peas are soft.
Remove the mint leaves and transfer soup to a blender. Puree until smooth.
Let it chill in the refrigerator until cold or serve immediately and enjoy!

Nutritional Information per serving Calories: 154 Fat: 3 g Carbohydrates: 22 g Protein: 9 g

Creamy Zucchini Coconut Milk Soup (Carbohydrates)

Servings: 4 servings

Serving size: 28 oz. of total soup

Ingredients
- 1 tbsp. olive oil
- ½ medium yellow onion
- 2 garlic cloves
- ½ red jalapeno pepper
- 3 cups packed grated zucchini
- 1 tbsp. fresh mint leaves
- ½ tsp. kosher salt plus more to taste
- ½ tsp. freshly ground black pepper plus more to taste
- 2 ¾ cups vegetable broth
- ¾ cup coconut milk

Directions Preheat a large saucepan to medium-low heat.
Mince the garlic cloves and mint leaves.
Add olive oil, chili pepper and onions to the pot, cooking until onions are soft, but not browned.
Add the garlic and cook for two more minutes.
Up the heat to medium and add the zucchini and mint leaves. Cook for five minutes or until zucchini is soft.

Add broth and bring to a boil. Lower heat to a simmer and cook for 10 more minutes.
Remove soup from heat and let rest for ten minutes before transferring to a blender.
Blend until almost smooth and reintroduce to the soup pan with the coconut milk and season with salt and pepper to taste.
Serve in bowls immediately for hot soup or let chill in the refrigerator for two hours and enjoy!

Nutritional Information per serving Calories: 102 Fat: 8 g Carbohydrates: 8 g Protein: 2 g

Quinoa Vegetable Soup

Servings: 6 servings   **Serving size: 28 oz. of soup**

Ingredients

- 3 tbsps. extra virgin olive oil
- 1 medium yellow or white onion
- 3 carrots
- 2 celery stalks
- 1 to 2 cups seasonal vegetables, like zucchini, yellow squash, bell pepper, sweet potatoes or butternut squash
- 6 garlic cloves
- ½ tsp. dried thyme
- 28 oz. diced tomatoes
- 1 cup quinoa, rinsed well in a fine mesh colander
- 4 cups vegetable broth
- 2 cups water
- 1 tsp. salt, more to taste
- 2 bay leaves
- A pinch of red pepper flakes
- Freshly ground black pepper
- 15 oz. of great northern beans or chickpeas, rinsed and drained
- 1 cup chopped fresh kale or collard greens, tough ribs removed
- 1 to 2 tsps. lemon juice, to taste

Directions Preheat soup pot over medium heat.
Chop the onions, celery stalks, seasonal vegetables, and garlic cloves.
Add the olive oil and chopped ingredients to the pot and stir until onions are translucent.
Add in the tomatoes, garlic, and thyme, and cook until fragrant, stirring often.
Add the quinoa, water, salt, bay leaves, and pepper flakes. Season with black pepper as desired.
Bring to a boil and lower to a simmer, partially covering the pot.
Simmer for 25 minutes, adding the chopped greens at the end and simmering for five more minutes until the greens have softened.
Remove pot from the heat and remove the bay leaves. Add the lemon juice and stir.
Season as desired with more lemon juice and salt and pepper.
Season as desired and serve into bowls. Enjoy!

Nutritional Information per serving Calories: 280 Fat: 10.3 g Carbohydrates: 40.8 g Protein: 9 g

Chickpea Noodle Soup

Servings: 6 servings   **Serving size: 28 oz. of soup**

Ingredients

- 2 tbsps. extra-virgin olive oil
- 1 medium yellow onion
- 1 cup of celery
- 1 cup of carrots
- ¼ tsp. salt, more to taste
- ½ tsp. ground turmeric
- ½ tsp. curry powder
- 1 bay leaf
- 1½ cups cooked chickpeas
- 8 oz. whole grain, gluten-free spiral pasta
- 2 tbsps. chopped fresh flat-leaf parsley, plus extra for garnish
- 8 cups vegetable broth
- Freshly ground black pepper, to taste

Directions Preheat the soup pot to medium heat.
Chop the celery, onions, and carrots to the appropriate size for soup.
Add the oil, salt, and chopped vegetables to the pot. Cook while stirring until onions are translucent.
Add turmeric and curry powder, stirring for 30 seconds. Add the broth, bay leaves, parsley, chickpeas, and pasta.
Raise heat to high and simmer for 10 to 20 minutes, stirring throughout until pasta is tender.
Remove the pot from the heat and add salt and pepper to taste if desired.

Nutritional Information per serving Calories: 312 Fat: 7.8 g Carbohydrates: 53.4 g Protein: 9 g

Macro Minestrone Soup

Servings: 6 servings **Serving size: 28 oz. of soup**

Ingredients
- 2 tbsps. olive oil
- 3 cloves garlic
- 1 onion
- 2 carrots
- 2 stalks celery
- 1½ tsps. dried basil
- 1 tsp. dried oregano
- ½ tsp. fennel seed
- 6 cups low sodium chicken broth
- 28 oz. can diced tomatoes
- 16 oz. can kidney beans, drained and rinsed
- 1 zucchini
- 1 (3-in.) Parmesan rind (remove for vegan variation)
- 1 bay leaf
- 1 bunch of kale
- 2 tsps. red wine vinegar
- Salt and freshly ground black pepper, to taste
- ¾ cup freshly grated Parmesan (remove for vegan variation)
- 2 tbsps. chopped fresh parsley leaves

Directions Preheat soup pot to medium heat.
Chop onions, zucchini, celery, and carrots to desired size for soup.
Mince the garlic cloves
Add olive oil, garlic, onions, celery and carrots to the pot. Cook for two to three minutes while stirring occasionally.
Add in basil, oregano, and fennel seeds, stirring until fragrant.
Pour in chicken stock and add tomatoes, kidney beans, zucchini, parmesan rind and bay leaf.
Simmer on low heat for 25 minutes, stirring throughout.
Add kale and simmer for another five minutes or until kale is wilted.
Add red wine vinegar and stir.
Season with salt and pepper to taste.
Serve in bowls, garnish with parmesan cheese, and enjoy!

Nutritional Information per serving Calories: 227 Fat: 7 g Carbohydrates: 26 g Protein: 14 g

Roasted Butternut Squash Soup

Servings: 4 servings **Serving size: 28 oz. of soup**

Ingredients
- 3 lbs. butternut squash
- 1 tbsp. olive oil, plus more for drizzling
- ½ cup shallots
- 1 tsp. of salt
- 4 garlic cloves
- 1 tsp. maple syrup
- A pinch of ground nutmeg
- Black pepper, to taste
- 3 to 4 cups of vegetable broth, as needed
- 1 to 2 tbsps. butter, to taste (replace with olive oil for vegan variation)

Directions Preheat the oven to 425° F
Cut the butternut squash vertically and remove the seeds.
Place butternut squash face down on an oven safe cooking tray with parchment paper, having olive oil spread throughout.
Bake butternut squash for 40 to 50 minutes, if the skin browns, that's fine.
As the squash bakes, preheat a saucepan to medium heat.
Chop the shallots and mince the garlic.
Add the shallots and the salt to the pan, stirring until shallots soften.
Add the garlic and cook until fragrant, stirring frequently.
Add the contents of the pan to a blender.
Using a large spoon, scoop out the squash and add to the blender, discarding the skin.
Add maple syrup, nutmeg, and ground black pepper to the blender.
Add the vegetable broth, and puree until smooth, warm, and creamy. Do this in batches if necessary.
If necessary, warm soup in a soup pot over medium heat.
Add butter or olive oil to taste.
Serve and enjoy!

Nutritional Information per serving Calories: 154 Fat: 6.8 g Carbohydrates: 24.3 g Protein: 2.7 g

Chapter 3: Salads

Salads and why they are Important

Salads, like soups, are a misunderstood dish category. It's easy to brush them off as side dishes or appetizers in a meal, or think of simple Caesar salads served in restaurants. These are not only unbalanced but they're also covered in fatty dressings with high sugar content. That's doing a disservice to salads as a whole because they have so much potential. The recipes listed here will help you understand more about this important food group.

The reason salads aren't respected is likely the same reason that vegetables aren't appreciated. Few people know how to prepare them properly or how to make salads that taste good. This shouldn't be a surprise, especially when you consider that many people use salads as a way to eat their vegetables. But that's all the more reason why they are essential. A good salad can cover all four main food groups of this diet and fill you up without making the experience horrible. This is also the most accessible food group to prepare because of the abundance of fresh ingredients necessary to make them and they require little to no use of stoves, ovens, or grills. It's also possible to keep dressings and the elements separate until it's time to eat them if you're planning on saving them for later. Whatever the case may be, it's not a good idea to skip out on salad recipes for the sake of not just the Macro diet but your taste buds.

The salads of this chapter are separated into protein-packed salads and lighter salads. The protein-packed salads feature salads with either animal or plant-based protein. They are intended for lunch or dinner meals. The lighter salads are meant for people looking to eat lighter meals or to avoid consuming heavy foods depending on the time of day and meal plan you're following for the diet. These categories are preceded by notes on dressings and how you should approach them or make your own. Either way, you'll be enjoying great salads often, thanks to these recipes!

Dressings

It's often difficult to make dressings at home due to various constraints which means relying on store-bought dressings to save time. So how should you approach dressings? The same way you approach the rest of the food in the Macro diet, by paying attention to the listed nutrition facts. The ideal salad dressings will meet the following requirements:

- Less than 250 milligrams of sodium per serving
- Less than 3 grams of added sugar per serving
- No artificial colors or preservatives
- Few to no vegetable oils

The key here is to avoid sugar and artificial preservatives as much as possible, as these can be detrimental to your health. Some of the recipes in this section of the cookbook will come with their own dressing recipes that are included in the final part of the nutritional information, but some people prefer different kinds of dressing and some of these dressings are meant to go with different kinds of salads. It's best to combine the salad dressing as you see fit, though recommendations will be included.

This should also be your thought process when making your own salad dressings. It's the same process used to create the salad dressings you see here.

Shopping List

- Salt
- Pepper
- Olive oil
- Red Wine Vinegar
- White Balsamic Vinegar
- Rice Vinegar
- Sesame Oil
- Grapeseed Oil
- Apple Cider Vinegar
- Honey
- Dijon Mustard
- Mayonnaise
- Ketchup
- Soy Sauce
- Miso
- Anchovy Paste
- Peanut Butter
- Coconut Aminos
- Tamari
- Tahini
- Clove Garlic
- Parsley
- Basil
- Oregano
- Onion Powder
- Garlic Powder
- Italian Seasonings
- Chives
- Ginger
- Cilantro
- Paprika
- Nutritional Yeast
- Milk
- Buttermilk
- Parmesan Cheese
- Blue Cheese
- Greek Yogurt
- Sour Cream
- Eggs
- Lemon
- Dill Pickles
- White Onion
- Carrot
- Avocado
- Eggplant

Classic Vinaigrette

Servings: 2 servings   **Serving size: One tbsp.**

Ingredients
- 2 tbsps. red wine vinegar
- 2 tbsps. olive oil
- Salt and Pepper to taste

Directions Whisk the oil and vinegar in a cup until mixed to proper consistency. Serve over a salad and add salt and pepper to taste. Enjoy!

Nutritional Information per serving Calories: 123 Fat: 14 g Carbohydrates: 0.1 g Protein: 0 g

Basil Vinaigrette

Servings: 4 servings   **Serving size: One tbsp.**

Ingredients
- ⅓ cup champagne wine vinegar can use red wine vinegar or white balsamic vinegar
- ½ clove garlic
- ¼ cup fresh parsley
- ¾ cup fresh basil
- ¾ cup lemon juice
- ¼ tsp. kosher salt
- ¼ tsp. fresh ground pepper
- 2 tbsps. honey
- 1 tbsp. olive oil
- 100 g non-fat Greek yogurt

Directions Blend all of the ingredients except the yogurt and olive oil in a blender until smooth, drizzling in olive oil as it blends.
Add the yogurt and blend until smooth.
Serve over a salad and enjoy!

Nutritional Information per serving Calories: 63 Fat: 3.7 g Carbohydrates: 4.3 g Protein: 2.9 g

Dijon Vinaigrette

Servings: 2 servings   **Serving size: One tbsp.**

Ingredients
- 2 tbsps. red wine vinegar
- 1 tsp. Dijon mustard
- ½ tsp. honey

Directions Mix all the ingredients in a bowl and stir to reach proper consistency. Serve and enjoy!

Nutritional Information per serving Calories: 21 Fat: 0 g Carbohydrates: 3 g

Macro Caesar Dressing

Servings: 15 servings   **Serving size: One tbsp.**

Ingredients
- 1 egg yolk
- 2 tsps. Dijon mustard
- 1 tbsp. anchovy paste
- 2 tbsps. lemon juice
- 2 cloves garlic
- 1 tbsp. oregano
- 1 tsp. salt
- 1 tsp. black pepper
- ½ cup of olive oil
- ½ cup parmesan cheese

Directions Place all the ingredients in a blender except the olive oil and pulse until smooth.
Pulse in the olive oil to achieve a thick consistency.
Serve over a salad and enjoy!

Nutritional Information per serving Calories: 114 Fat: 11.7 g Carbohydrates: 1.1 g Protein: 5.2 g

Macro Blue Cheese Dressing

Servings: 16 servings **Serving size: One tbsp.**

Ingredients
- 1 cup mayonnaise
- ½ cup sour cream
- 4 oz. blue cheese crumbles
- 1 tsp. lemon juice
- ¼ cup unsweetened almond milk (or any milk of choice)
- ½ tsp. sea salt (to taste)
- ¼ tsp. black pepper (to taste)

Directions Stir all ingredients in a bowl, crushing the blue cheese crumbles to incorporate their flavor.
Serve in a salad and enjoy!

Nutritional Information per serving Calories: 99 Fat: 8.1/2 g Carbohydrates: 4.4 g Protein: 1.6 g

Macro Thousand Island Dressing

Servings: 12 servings **Serving size: One tbsp.**

Ingredients
- 1 cup mayonnaise
- ¼ cup sugar-free ketchup
- 2 tbsps. apple cider vinegar
- 2 tbsps. no sugar added sweetener
- 1 ½ tbsps. dill pickles (finely chopped)
- 2 tsps. white onion (minced)
- ¼ tsp. sea salt
- ⅛ tsp. black pepper

Directions Mix together all ingredients in a bowl, stirring to reach dressing consistency.
Serve in a salad and enjoy!

Nutritional Information per serving Calories: 87 Fat: 6.5 g Carbohydrates: 7 g Protein: 0.5 g

Macro Ranch Dressing

Servings: 16 servings **Serving size: One tbsp.**

Ingredients
- 1 tbsp. dried parsley
- 2 tsps. garlic powder
- 2 tsps. onion powder
- ¼ tsp. ground black pepper
- ½ tsp. salt
- 1 tbsp. fresh chives
- 1 cup nonfat plain Greek yogurt
- ¾ cup buttermilk
- 1 tsp. Dijon mustard
- 1 tsp. lemon juice

Directions Pulse the parsley and chives in a blender until they reach a flake shape.
Using a spatula, put the herbs on the sides of the bowl down to avoid them sticking to the sides.
Add all remaining ingredients to the blender and pulse until fully incorporated, using the spatula to reincorporate the herbs if necessary.
Serve over a salad and enjoy!

Nutritional Information per serving Calories: 87 Fat: 6.5 g Carbohydrates: 7 g Protein: 0.5 g

Macro Italian Dressing

Servings: 16 servings **Serving size: One tbsp.**

Ingredients
- ¾ cup olive oil
- ¼ cup white wine vinegar
- ½ tbsp. no sugar added sweetener
- 2 tsps. Italian seasoning
- 1 tsp. garlic powder
- ½ tsp. onion powder
- ¾ tsp. sea salt
- ¼ tsp. black pepper

Directions Mix all the ingredients in a bowl and whisk.
Serve over a salad and enjoy!

Nutritional Information per serving Calories: 169 Fat: 19.3 g Carbohydrates: 0.6 g Protein: 0.1 g

Macro Peanut Dressing

Servings: 20 servings **Serving size: One tbsp.**

Ingredients
- ½ cup smooth, all natural peanut butter
- ¼ cup lime juice
- 1 tbsp. soy sauce
- 1 tbsp. ginger
- 2 tsps. toasted sesame oil
- 2 garlic cloves
- ½ cup water
- Sea salt, to taste

Directions Mince the garlic cloves and ginger.
Mix all the ingredients in a bowl, thinning with water to attain dressing consistency as needed.
Serve over a salad and enjoy!

Nutritional Information per serving Calories:45 Fat: 3.8 g Carbohydrates: 0.6 g Protein: 1.5 g

Macro Ginger Dressing

Servings: 28 servings **Serving size: One tbsp.**

Ingredients
- 2 carrots
- 1 tbsp. ginger
- ¾ cup rice vinegar
- ½ cup grapeseed oil
- ¼ cup sesame oil
- 1 tbsp. nutritional yeast
- 1 tsp. coconut aminos or tamari
- 1 tsp. honey
- ½ tsp. miso
- Pinch of Kosher salt and black pepper

Directions Cut the carrots and ginger into large chunks for blending.
Add all the ingredients except the oil to the blender and blend slowly until the ingredients are mixed
Add the oil in increments and blend to stir.
Serve over a salad and enjoy!

Nutritional Information per serving Calories:58 Fat: 5.9 g Carbohydrates: 1 g Protein: 0.2 g

Macro Avocado Dressing

Servings: 8 servings **Serving size: Two tbsps.**

Ingredients
- 1 avocado
- ¼ cup olive oil
- ¼ cup water, or more for thinner consistency
- ¼ cup fresh cilantro
- 1 juice from one lime
- 2 garlic cloves
- Salt and pepper, to taste

Directions Mince the garlic and herbs.
Peel and remove the seed from the avocado.
Mash the avocado into a sauce consistency and stir it, alongside all the other ingredients in a bowl.
Serve over a salad and enjoy!

Nutritional Information per serving Calories: 83 Fat: 9 g Carbohydrates: 2 g Protein: 0.2 g

Baba Ghanouj Dressing

Servings: 4 servings **Serving size: One tbsp.**

Ingredients
- 2 medium eggplants
- ¼ cup tahini
- 3 tbsps. fresh lemon juice
- 2 tbsps. extra virgin olive oil
- 2 garlic cloves
- ½ tsp. sea salt
- 1 dash smoked paprika
- Water as needed for thinning.

Directions Preheat oven to 400º F.
Puncture the eggplants in various places with a fork to prevent exploding while baking.
Wrap the eggplant in foil.
Bake for 40-50 minutes.
Once the eggplant is cool, remove the skin and halve, removing all the seeds.
Place the eggplant in a strainer pot and set in water for 20 minutes.
Mix all the ingredients in a blender, adding in water as needed for desired consistency.
Serve and enjoy!

Nutritional Information per serving Calories: 212 Fat: 15.6 g Carbohydrates: 17.4 g Protein: 5 g

Protein-Packed Salads

Shopping List

- Romaine lettuce
- Baby arugula
- Spinach
- Artichoke hearts
- Avocado
- Cucumber
- Tomatoes
- Carrot
- Green bell pepper
- Yellow bell peppers
- Red bell peppers
- Roasted red pepper
- Banana peppers
- Red onion
- Green onion
- Shallot
- Scallions
- Eggplant
- Asparagus
- Celery stalk
- Pumpkin
- Black olives
- Kalamata olives
- Green beans
- White beans
- Chickpeas
- Garbanzo beans
- Kidney beans
- Red beans
- Wax beans
- Strawberries
- Mango
- Watermelon
- Dried cranberries
- Eggs
- Applewood smoked ham
- Chicken
- Ground beef
- Tofu
- Bulgur
- Canned tuna
- Salami
- pepperoni
- Pepperoncini
- Cheddar cheese
- Gorgonzola cheese
- Feta cheese
- Blue cheese
- Mozzarella balls
- Butter
- Walnuts
- Pine nuts
- Watercress
- Canned hearts of palm
- Canned tomato sauce
- Wheat penne
- Hot sauce
- Cornstarch
- Pickle chips

Macro Cobb Salad

Servings: 1 serving

Ingredients
- 2 cups chopped Romaine lettuce
- 1 hard-boiled egg
- ¼ avocado
- 1 rotisserie chicken breast
- 1 oz. applewood smoked ham (chopped)
- ½ cup chopped cucumber
- ½ cup chopped tomatoes
- Dressing recommendation: Dijon Vinaigrette

Directions Chop the chicken and avocado to bite-size slices, making sure to remove the bones and skin from the chicken. Mix all the ingredients on a plate.
Serve with chosen dressing and enjoy!

Nutritional Information (without dressing) per serving Calories: 478 Fat: 13.4 g Carbohydrates: 8.1 g Protein: 78 g

Macro Chicken Caesar Salad

Servings: 1 serving

Ingredients
- 1 head Romaine lettuce
- 2 cups grape tomatoes
- 2 large chicken breasts
- Dressing Recommendation: Macro Caesar Dressing

Directions Remove the skin and bones from the chicken breasts and cut into long slices.
Grill or oven-roast the chicken breasts until fully cooked.
Halve the grape tomatoes, removing the stems. Chop the romaine lettuce until bite sized.
Toss all the ingredients together with the dressing.
Serve and enjoy!

Nutritional Information (Without Dressing) per serving Calories: 495 Fat: 16.6 g Carbohydrates: 23.7 g Protein: 63.1 g

Roast Turkey Salad

Servings: 4 serving **Serving size: 28 oz. of salad**

Ingredients
- 1 lb. baby arugula
- 2 cups turkey breast cooked and chopped
- 6 oz. gorgonzola crumbles
- ¾ cup dried cranberries
- ½ cup walnut halves
- Dressing Recommendation: Classic or Basil Vinaigrette

Directions Remove the skin and bones from the turkey breasts and cut into long slices.
Grill or oven-roast the turkey breasts until fully cooked, keeping them marinated in their juices with a brush or baster to avoid drying out. Toss all the ingredients together with the dressing.
Serve and enjoy!

Nutritional Information per serving Calories: 567 Fat: 29.1/2 g Carbohydrates: 6.1/2 g Protein: 63.6 g

Hard-Boiled Egg Salad

Servings: 4 servings **Serving size: 28 oz. of salad**

Ingredients
- 8 eggs
- 2 cups spinach leaves
- 2 cups green beans
- 1 medium cucumber
- 1 cup cherry tomatoes
- Dressing Recommendation: Classic Vinaigrette

Directions Preheat a pan to medium heat.
Submerge the eggs in a separate pan of water.
Bring the pan with the eggs to a boil, let them boil for nine to 12 minutes.
While waiting for the eggs to boil, add water to the separate pan and steam the green beans for one to two minutes, until crisp.
Peel and slice the cucumber into bite-size slices.
Remove the shells from the eggs. Halve the tomatoes and the eggs.
Toss the salad with your chosen dressing, serve and enjoy!

Nutritional Information (Without Dressing) per serving Calories: 206 Fat: 10.1 g Carbohydrates: 14.1 g Protein: 16.3 g

Hamburger Salad

Servings: 2 servings **Serving size: 28 oz. of salad**

Ingredients
- For the burgers:
- 8 oz. ground beef
- 1 tsp. Worcestershire sauce
- ½ tsp. garlic powder
- ½ tsp. onion powder
- ½ tsp. seasoned salt
- Cooking spray to avoid sticking.
- For the salad:
- 3 cups mixed greens of your choice
- ½ cup grated cheddar cheese
- ½ cup of grape tomatoes
- ¼ cup dill pickle chips
- Recommended Dressing: Macro Avocado Dressing

Directions Preheat a pan to medium heat.
Mix all the meat ingredients together in a bowl.
Spray the pan with cooking spray and add meat, stirring until brown.
Remove the stems from the tomatoes and half them. Add all the ingredients to a bowl and toss with dressing until fully mixed. Serve and enjoy!

Nutritional Information (Without Dressing) per serving Calories: 515 Fat: 17 g Carbohydrates: 39 g Protein: 49.7 g

Buffalo Chicken Salad

Servings: 4 servings **Serving size: 28 oz. of salad**

Ingredients
For the Chicken:
- 10 oz. white meat chicken.
- 3 tbsps. of butter
- ¼ cup of hot sauce

For the Salad:
- 1 large romaine lettuce bunch
- 1 small carrot
- ¼ cup banana peppers
- 4 scallions
- ½ cup cherry tomatoes
- ¼ cup crumbled blue cheese
- 1 large avocado
- Suggested Dressing: Macro Blue Cheese or Macro Ranch

Directions Preheat a saucepan to medium heat.
Skin and debone the chicken and cut into bite-size pieces.
Melt the butter in the pan and add the chicken, cooking fully.
Toss the chicken in the hot sauce.
Chop the romaine lettuce to bite-size pieces. Chop the scallions into small pieces.
Remove the stems from the tomatoes and halve them.
Toss all the ingredients and desired dressing together in a large bowl.
Serve and enjoy!

Nutritional Information (Without Dressing) per serving Calories: 360 Fat: 23.2 g Carbohydrates: 14 g Protein: 25.3 g

Vegan/Vegetarian

Tofu Ginger Salad

Servings: 4 servings **Serving size: 28 oz. of salad**

Ingredients

For the Tofu:
- 1 block (14 oz.) extra firm tofu
- 1 tbsp. soy sauce
- 1 tbsp. cornstarch
- 1 tsp. vegan Worcestershire sauce

For the Salad:
- ½ cup white beans
- ½ cup chickpeas
- ½ cup red beans
- 2½ oz. spring mix or greens of your choice.
- 1 cup diced tomato
- ½ cup diced yellow bell pepper
- Recommended Dressing: Macro Ginger Dressing or Macro Peanut Dressing.

Directions Press the tofu to remove moisture.
Preheat the oven to 425° F.
Cut the tofu into bite-size cubes. Put the tofu cubes in a bowl, mixing in the soy sauce, vegan Worcestershire sauce, and cornstarch with a spatula. Put the tofu slices on a baking tray with parchment paper.
Bake for 25-30 minutes, until the tofu is crispy.
Remove tofu from the oven and set aside to cool.
Toss all the ingredients and chosen salad dressing together.
Serve and enjoy!

Nutritional Information (Without Dressing) per serving Calories: 349 Fat: 6.2 g Carbohydrates: 52.3 g Protein: 25.9 g

Three Bean Salad

Servings: 16 servings **Serving size: 28 oz. of salad**

Ingredients
- 15 oz. canned green beans
- 1 lb. canned wax beans
- 15 oz. canned kidney beans
- 1 onion
- ¾ cup of white sugar
- ⅔ cup of distilled white vinegar
- ¾ cup of vegetable oil
- ½ tsp. salt
- ½ tsp. ground black pepper
- ½ tsp. celery seed

Directions Wash and rinse the beans overnight to soften them.
Chop the onion into small rings.
Mix the ingredients in a large bowl, stirring with a spatula.
Cover the bowl with plastic and place in the refrigerator for at least 12 hours.
Serve into bowls and enjoy!

Nutritional Information (Dressing Included) per serving Calories: 111.1/2 Fat: 4.7 g Carbohydrates: 15.9 g Protein: 2 g

Garlic Garbanzo Salad

Servings: 16 servings   **Serving size: 28 oz. of salad**

Ingredients
- ¼ cup fresh rosemary
- 5 cloves garlic (about 4 tbsps.)
- 1 cup fresh parsley
- 2 tbsps. olive oil
- 3 tbsps. fresh lemon juice
- 30 oz. canned garbanzo beans
- Salt and pepper to taste

Directions Drain and rinse the garbanzo beans, soaking them in water overnight.
Chop the rosemary and parsley finely. Mince the garlic cloves.
Mix all the ingredients together in a large bowl.
Serve immediately or save up to three days in the refrigerator. Enjoy!

Nutritional Information (No dressing) per serving Calories: 111.5 Fat: 4.7 g Carbohydrates: 15.9 g Protein: 2 g

Cooked Eggplant Salad

Servings: 12 servings   **Serving size: 28 oz. of salad**

Ingredients
- 2 large eggplants
- 6 tbsps. olive oil
- 2 red or yellow bell peppers, or one of each.
- 4 cloves of garlic
- 15 oz. canned tomato sauce
- 1 cup of water
- 1 tsp. of cumin
- 1 tsp. of salt
- 1 tsp. sugar
- ½ tsp. crushed red pepper flakes
- ¼ tsp. black pepper

Directions Preheat a saucepan and large pot to low heat.
Peel the eggplants, removing the skins and green stems. Cut the eggplant into bite-size pieces.
Seed and cut the peppers into small pieces. Mince the garlic cloves.
Add olive oil and eggplants to the pan and cook for ten minutes. You may need to do this in increments. Repeat with the bell peppers, adding in the onions during the last two minutes with the bell peppers.
Transfer the eggplant and peppers to the large pot when finished cooking.
In a separate large bowl, mix the tomato sauce, water, cumin, salt, sugar, crushed red pepper flakes and black pepper until fully integrated.
Put the mix in the bowl into the pot and bring to a boil.
Reduce heat to medium-low and partially cover to allow venting.
Simmer for one hour and serve in bowls. Enjoy!

Nutritional Information (No Dressing) per serving Calories: 99 Fat: 7 g Carbohydrates: 8 g Protein: 1 g

Macro Falafel Salad

Servings: 4 servings   **Serving size: 28 oz. of salad**

Ingredients
- 1 bunch (¼ cup) flat leaf parsley
- 1 bunch (¼ cup) cilantro
- 19 oz. can of chickpeas
- ½ cup uncooked bulgur
- 2 tomatoes
- 1 cup of water
- Recommended dressing: Baba Ghanouj Dressing

Directions Drain and rinse the chickpeas, letting them soak overnight in a bowl.
Preheat a saucepan to medium heat.
Place the bulgur in the saucepan and toast while stirring for two minutes.
Add the water to the pan and bring to a boil. Lower the heat and let simmer for 20 minutes.
Transfer the bulgur to the refrigerator uncovered to cool.
Finely chop the parsley and cilantro and add to a large bowl. Dice the tomatoes and add to the bowl.
Drain the water used to soak the chickpeas and add them to the bowl.
Add the cooled bulgur and chosen dressing. Toss with a spatula to mix all ingredients.
Serve in bowls and enjoy!

Nutritional Information (Without Dressing) per serving Calories: 565 Fat: 8.5 g Carbohydrates: 98.2 g Protein: 29.1 g

Tuna Salad

Servings: 1

Ingredients
- ½ cup of canned tuna in oil
- 1 avocado
- 1 mango
- Recommended Dressing: Dijon Vinaigrette

Directions Peel and remove the seeds from the mango and avocado.
Slice the avocado and mango into bite-size pieces.
Drain the oil from the tuna and crumble it over the bowl.
Add chosen dressing, serve and enjoy!

Nutritional Information (Without Dressing) per serving Calories: 765 Fat: 46.5 g Carbohydrates: 67.6 g Protein: 27.8 g

Lighter Salads

Strawberry Asparagus Salad

Servings: 7   **Serving size: 28 oz.**

Ingredients
- 1 lb. fresh asparagus, trimmed and cut into 1-in. pieces
- 3 tbsps. olive oil, divided
- ¼ tsp. salt
- ¼ tsp. coarsely ground pepper
- 8 cups spring mix salad greens
- 3 cups sliced fresh strawberries
- ¼ small red onion
- 1/4 cup chopped walnuts
- 2 tbsps. balsamic vinegar

Directions Preheat the oven to 400º F.
Rinse the asparagus and cut them into one-inch pieces.
Toss the asparagus in a bowl with olive oil and place on a baking tray with parchment paper.
Bake the asparagus for 15-20 minutes, or until tender.
While asparagus is baking, preheat a skillet pan to medium heat.
Cut the onion into thin slices.
Remove the stems from the strawberries and cut them into bite-size pieces.
Toast the walnuts in the skillet pan for one to two minutes or until fragrant.
Whisk the oil and vinegar together for dressing and toss with all ingredients in a large bowl.
Serve and enjoy!

Nutritional Information (Dressing Included) per serving Calories: 280 Fat: 11.6 g Carbohydrates: 45.3 g Protein: 13.2 g

Macro Garden Salad

Servings: 4 **Serving size: 28 oz.**

Ingredients
- 24 cups mixed salad greens
- 1 red onion
- 1 Celery stalk
- 1 cucumber
- 1 cup cherry tomatoes
- Recommended dressing: Classic Vinaigrette

Directions Wash and rinse all the vegetables under cold water.
Peel and chop the onion and cucumber to bite-size portions.
Chop the celery stalk to bite-size portions. Halve the cherry tomatoes.
Mix all the ingredients and chosen dressing in a large bowl.
Serve and enjoy!

Nutritional Information (Without Dressing) per serving Calories: 79.6 Fat: 0.3 g Carbohydrates: 16.7 g Protein: 4.4 g

Seasonal Pumpkin Salad

Servings: 4 **Serving size: 28 oz.**

Ingredients
- 1 lb. 4 oz. pumpkin
- 1 tbsp. olive oil
- 2 oz. Feta Cheese
- 1 Avocado
- 2 cups Spinach Leaves
- 1 cup of almonds
- Recommended dressing: Macro Ginger Dressing or Macro Peanut Dressing

Directions Preheat the oven to 300º F.
Slice the pumpkin into small, bite-size slices.
Place the slices on a baking tray lined with parchment paper and brush olive oil over the pumpkin slices.
Bake the slices for ten minutes, flip them, brush with more olive oil and bake for another ten minutes.
Chop the almonds to bite-size shapes.
Toss all ingredients in a large bowl with chosen dressing.
Serve and enjoy!

Nutritional Information (Without Dressing) per serving Calories: 364 Fat: 28.9 g Carbohydrates: 22.7 g Protein: 10.2 g

Carrot Salad

Servings: 4   **Serving size: 28 oz.**

Ingredients
- 3 tbsps. olive oil
- 1 lb. of carrots
- 2 green onions
- 3 tbsps. parsley
- Recommended Dressing: Dijon Vinaigrette

Directions Wash the carrots, parsley, and the green onions under cold water.
Finely chop the parsley and green onions. Julienne the carrots to thin strands.
Toss all ingredients in a large bowl with chosen dressing.
Serve and enjoy!

Nutritional Information per serving Calories: 140 Fat: 1.5 g Carbohydrates: 11.9 g Protein: 1.2 g

Fresh Watermelon Salad

Servings: 4   **Serving size: 28 oz.**

Ingredients
- 5 cups watermelon
- 1 cup cucumber
- ¼ cup of red onions
- ¾ cup of crumbled feta cheese
- 1 avocado
- ⅓ cup mint or basil leaves
- Sea salt to taste.
- Recommended dressing: Classic Vinaigrette.

Directions Peel and dice the onion, avocado and cucumber.
Finely chop the mint or basil leaves.
Chop the watermelon to bite-size pieces, removing any visible seeds.
Toss with chosen dressing and serve in a bowl. Enjoy!

Nutritional Information per serving Calories: 200 Fat: 12.7 g Carbohydrates: 21 g Protein: 4.2 g

Watercress and Hearts of Palm Salad

Servings: 4   **Serving size: 28 oz.**

Ingredients
- 2 cups of watercress
- 1 avocado
- 1 cup canned hearts of palm
- 2 tbsps. pine nuts
- Recommended Dressing: Basil vinaigrette

Directions Drain and rinse the hearts of palm and watercress in a strainer using cold water.
Peel and remove the seed from the avocado. Chop it into bite-size portions.
Chop the watercress to bite-size portions. Toss all ingredients in a large bowl with chosen dressing.

Nutritional Information per serving Calories: 145 Fat: 13.1 g Carbohydrates: 6.6 g Protein: 3 g

Artichoke Heart Salad

Servings: 1

Ingredients
- 1 cup grape tomatoes
- 4 cups packaged arugula

- 1 ½ cups canned artichoke hearts
- ½ cup canned roasted red peppers
- Recommended Dressing: Macro Italian Dressing

Directions Strain the artichoke hearts and roasted peppers to remove excess oil.
Halve the tomatoes and remove their stems.
Rinse the arugula in cold water.
Toss all ingredients and chosen salad dressing in a large bowl.
Serve and enjoy!

Nutritional Information per serving Calories: 126 Fat: 0.8 g Carbohydrates: 23.1 g Protein: 6.5 g

Antipasto Pasta Salad

Servings: 8   **Serving size: 1 cup**

Ingredients
- 8 cups chopped romaine lettuce
- ¾ cup grape or cherry tomatoes, halved
- 6 oz. provolone cheese
- 4 oz. canned marinated artichokes hearts
- ½ cup black olives
- 2 oz. salami, diced
- 2 oz. pepperoni, quartered
- ¼ cup sliced pepperoncinis
- ¼ cup sliced red onion
- Recommended Dressing: Macro Italian Dressing

Directions Drain the artichoke hearts and olives in separate strainers to remove excess liquid.
Rinse the romaine lettuce. Chop the provolone cheese into bite-size chunks. Toss all ingredients in a large bowl with chosen dressing.

Nutritional Information (Without Dressing) per serving Calories: 157 Fat: 11.4 g Carbohydrates: 5.3 g Protein: 8.9 g

Macro Greek Salad

Servings: 4   **Serving size: 28 oz.**

Ingredients
- 1 cucumber
- 1 green bell pepper
- 2 cups halved cherry tomatoes
- 5 oz. feta cheese
- ¾ cup thinly sliced red onion
- ¾ cup pitted Kalamata olives
- ¾ cup fresh mint leaves
- Recommended Dressing: Basil Vinaigrette

Directions Rinse all the vegetables in cold water.
Peel and chop the onion and cucumber into bite-size pieces.
Drain the excess liquid of the Kalamata olives in a strainer. Chop the mint leaves finely.
Mix all ingredients in a large bowl and toss with your chosen salad dressing.

Nutritional Information (Without Dressing) per serving Calories: 156 Fat: 9 g Carbohydrates: 13.7 g Protein: 7.3 g

Spinach and Arugula Salad

Servings: 2	**Serving size: Half of total salad**

Ingredients
- 4 oz. spinach
- 4 oz. arugula
- ¾ cup of lemon juice
- 1 tbsp. of olive oil
- Salt and pepper to taste
- ¼ cup of shredded parmesan cheese
- Recommended Dressings: Classic Vinaigrette, Basil vinaigrette, Macro Italian Dressing

Directions Mix all ingredients in a large bowl with chosen dressing.

Nutritional Information (Without Dressing) per serving Calories: 187 Fat: 13.9 g Carbohydrates: 6 g Protein: 12.4 g

Macro Caprese Salad

Servings: 5	**Serving size: 28 oz.**

Ingredients
- 5 large tomatoes, sliced
- ½ lb. fresh mozzarella balls, drained and sliced
- ½ cup fresh basil leaves
- 1 tbsp. lemon juice
- 2 tsps. dry white wine
- 3 tbsps. extra-virgin olive oil
- ½ tsp. fine sea salt
- ½ tsp. ground black pepper

Directions Alternate cheese, basil leaves, and tomatoes on a large serving plate.
Whisk the wine, lemon juice, and salt and pepper in a bowl. Add the oil and whisk gently.
Drizzle over the salad and wait ten minutes for ingredients to absorb dressing.

Nutritional Information (Dressing included) per serving Calories: 228 Fat: 17.8 g Carbohydrates: 7.4 g Protein: 11.7 g

Strawberry Caprese Salad

Servings: 4 servings	**Serving size: 28 oz. of salad**

Ingredients
- 8 oz. whole wheat penne
- ¼ cup white balsamic vinegar
- ¼ cup of mint.
- 2 tbsps. of olive oil
- ½ small shallot
- 12 oz. strawberries
- 4 oz. pearl mozzarella, halving if large
- A pinch each of salt and pepper

Directions Prepare the pasta as stated on the box.
As the water is boiling for the pasta, chop the mint and shallot into small pieces.
Whisk the shallots and mint with the salt, pepper, olive oil, and vinegar in a large bowl.
When the pasta is ready, rinse it under cold water to chill it.
Remove the stems from the strawberries and chop them into bite-size pieces.
Add all ingredients except the mint into the large bowl and toss until mixed.
Serve into bowls and top with mint. Enjoy!

Nutritional Information (Dressing included) per serving Calories: 402 Fat: 15.1/2 g Carbohydrates: 53 g Protein: 13 g

Chapter 4: Sandwiches and Wraps

Sandwiches, Wraps, and Versatility

With all the talk about fast and slow carbohydrates in chapter one, it's almost ludicrous to think that an entire chapter focuses on fast carbohydrates rather than slow ones. There is a good reason for this, however. First, you must remember that sandwiches and wraps can be made using whole-grain bread and wraps, which are slower carbohydrates than refined grains like white bread and white wraps. Next, a reminder that chapter one also explained that fast carbohydrates are used up when exercising. Remember, balance is the key to the entire diet. As long as you're exercising and approaching your carbohydrates or any other food with caution, you'll succeed in what you're trying to do.

It's important to note that sandwiches and wraps are easy to make and transport as food, just like soups and salads. This section is perfect for people who don't have time to think about complex meals or what they're going to eat throughout the day. And the best part about this is that so long as you follow the diet rules and maintain a balance, your sandwich garnishes can be just about anything you want. That's not to say you shouldn't try the recipes listed here, as they already achieved that balance. Still, there's nothing wrong with exchanging black olives for peppers or adding both if you think that will create the meal you're looking for.

This chapter is separated into cold sandwiches, which are perfect for transporting and enjoying. The next focus is on hot sandwiches, which are perfect to enjoy during a more relaxed time. They require freshly cooked ingredients. The chapter will close with wraps, which are also simple to transport, and will focus on cold recipes more than hot ones.

Shopping List

- Fresh white bread
- Whole wheat sandwich bread
- Whole-grain sandwich bread
- Rye bread
- Cuban bread
- Ciabatta bread
- Kaiser bread
- Baguette
- Whole wheat bagel
- Whole wheat hamburger buns
- Whole wheat hot dog buns
- Sweet bread
- Whole wheat tortilla
- Flour tortilla
- Pita bread
- Pita flatbread
- Multigrain flatbread
- Brown rice
- All-purpose flour
- Panko breadcrumbs
- Ham
- Turkey
- Roast beef
- Bacon
- Eggs
- Prosciutto
- Salami
- Roast pork
- Chimichurri
- Beef chuck roast
- Ground beef
- Ground turkey
- Turkey sausage
- Ground lamb
- Canned white tuna
- Jumbo shrimp
- Shredded lettuce
- Arugula
- Tomato
- Spinach
- Carrot
- Avocado
- Cucumber
- Red onion
- Onion
- Alfalfa sprouts
- Celery
- Romaine lettuce
- Iceberg lettuce
- Dill pickle
- Yellow pepper
- Red pepper
- Chipotle chili
- Portobello mushrooms
- Black beans
- Capers
- Lime
- Lemon
- Mango
- Apples
- Sharp cheddar
- Provolone
- Cottage cheese
- Goat cheese
- Pepper jack
- Havarti cheese
- Swiss cheese
- Monterey jack cheese
- Comte cheese
- Fontina cheese
- Parmesan cheese
- Sour cream
- Greek yogurt
- Butter
- Milk
- Mayonnaise
- Mustard
- Dijon mustard
- Ketchup
- Hot sauce
- Horseradish
- Pesto sauce
- Salsa
- Hummus
- Coleslaw mix
- Olive oil

- Canola oil
- Coconut oil
- Balsamic vinegar
- Worcestershire sauce
- Adobo sauce
- Sauerkraut
- Beef broth
- Onion soup
- Light beer
- Salt
- Pepper
- Basil
- Cilantro
- Oregano
- Paprika
- Cayenne
- Cumin
- Chili powder
- Coriander
- Thyme
- Red pepper flakes
- Parsley
- Rosemary
- Cajun seasoning
- Taco seasoning
- Walnuts
- Raisins

Cold Sandwiches

Macro Italian Sub

Servings: 4 servings   **Serving size: One quarter of total sandwich**

Ingredients
- 1 baguette (410g)
- 8 oz. pesto sauce
- 3 oz. provolone cheese, thin sliced
- 11 oz. Black Forest ham, thin sliced
- 2 oz. prosciutto, thin sliced
- 2 oz. salami, thin sliced
- Shredded lettuce as desired
- 1 cup of tomato slices
- Macro Italian Dressing, if desired.

Directions Cut the bread down the middle, and place with the crust down.
Spread the pesto across both sides of the bread with a spoon or basting brush.
Place the cheese on one half of the bread, and layer the meats on the other.
Top with the tomato slices, lettuce, and dressing. Cut into fourths, serve and enjoy!

Nutritional Information per serving Calories: 490 Fat: 17 g Carbohydrates: 47.3 g Protein: 35.7 g

Hummus and Vegetable sandwich

Servings: 2 servings

Ingredients
- 4 pieces hearty whole grain sandwich bread
- 2 tbsps. Hummus
- ½ cup fresh spinach leaves
- 1 large carrot, grated
- 4 large ripe tomato slices
- 1 ripe avocado, sliced
- One red onion, thinly sliced
- ½ cup of Alfalfa sprouts
- Salt and pepper to taste

Directions For one sandwich, start by preparing all the vegetables as listed above.
Spread the hummus on each layer of the bread, making sure it's coated well.
Put a thin layer of spinach leaves on the sandwich. Add the vegetables and salt and pepper to taste.
Serve and enjoy!

Nutritional Information per serving Calories: 324 Fat: 14.2 g Carbohydrates: 38.4 g Protein: 12.1 g

Tuna Salad Sub

Servings: 4 servings   **Serving size: One sandwich**

Ingredients
- 12 oz. unsalted white tuna packed in water, drained
- ½ cup diced celery
- 1 tsp. lemon juice
- ¾ cup fat-free mayonnaise
- 4 romaine lettuce leaves, chopped
- 8 slices whole wheat bread

Directions Prepare the vegetables as listed above.
Flake the tuna with the fork, being careful to remove any bones.
Add the celery, mayonnaise, and lime juice, and mix until fully incorporated.
Serve in between two pieces of bread and the lettuce. Enjoy!

Nutritional Information per serving Calories: 490 Fat: 5 g Carbohydrates: 25 g Protein: 35.7 g

Macro Avocado Toast

Servings: 2 servings **Serving size: One sandwich**

Ingredients
- ½ ripe avocado
- ⅓ cup of 1% cottage cheese
- 1 tbsp. fresh-squeezed lime juice
- 2 slices of whole-wheat toast
- A pinch of sea salt
- A pinch of black pepper

Directions Toast the bread as desired.
In a bowl, mash the avocado with the cottage cheese.
Add the lemon juice, salt, and pepper and incorporate with the other ingredients.
Spread the mixture over the toasted bread and enjoy!

Nutritional Information per serving Calories: 224 Fat: 8 g Carbohydrates: 28 g Protein: 10 g

Spicy Roast Beef Sub

Servings: 2 servings **Serving size: One sandwich**

Ingredients
- 2 slices rye bread
- 1 tbsp. Macro Italian dressing
- 2 tbsps. mayonnaise, low sodium, low calorie or diet
- 1 cup, sliced cucumber, peeled, raw
- 2 tsps. horseradish, prepared
- ½ cup spinach, raw
- ½ lb. of roast beef

Directions Prepare the cucumber as said above.
Combine the horseradish and mayonnaise in a large bowl.
Toast the bread as desired. Spread the mayonnaise mix across the slices of bread.
Cut the cucumbers into small slices, and layer the ingredients on the sandwich.
Serve and enjoy!

Nutritional Information per serving Calories: 224 Fat: 8 g Carbohydrates: 28 g Protein: 10 g

Cucumber and Avocado Sandwich

Servings: 4 servings **Serving size: One sandwich**

Ingredients
- 8 slices whole wheat bread
- 8 oz. herbed goat cheese at room temperature
- 4 Romaine lettuce leaves washed and dried, chopped for sandwiches
- 1 large cucumber peeled and sliced for sandwiches
- 2 large avocados peeled, pitted, and sliced for sandwiches
- 2 tsps. of fresh lemon juice
- 1 cup alfalfa sprouts, rinsed and chopped
- Salt and black pepper to taste

Directions Prepare all the vegetables as listed above.
Spread the goat cheese on each slice of bread.
Take one of the slices of bread and add the lettuce, cucumber slices, and avocado slices.
Drizzle the lemon juice over the toppings. Add some sprouts and season with salt and black pepper, to taste.
Place the other slice of the bread with the cheese facing down on the sandwich.
Serve and enjoy!

Nutritional Information per serving Calories: 549 Fat: 29.1/2 g Carbohydrates: 54.2 g Protein: 23.1 g

Egg Salad Sub

Servings: 1 serving   **Serving size: One sandwich**

Ingredients
- 2 slices of whole wheat bread
- 2 large, whole, fresh eggs
- 2 tbsps. light mayonnaise
- 2 tsps. Dijon mustard
- A dash of salt and pepper

Directions Fill enough water in a large pot to fully submerge the eggs, but don't put them in yet.
Bring water to a boil and then carefully place eggs in the hot water.
Boil the eggs for 30 seconds, place a lid on the pot and reduce heat to low.
Cook eggs on a low simmer for 12 minutes.
Allow the eggs to chill in cold water before peeling and slicing them to the appropriate size for salad.
Mix the eggs and all other ingredients in a bowl, mixing until incorporated.
Spread the salad between the bread, serve, and enjoy!

Nutritional Information per serving Calories: 366 Fat: 19 g Carbohydrates: 28 g Protein: 20 g

Turkey Avocado Bagel

Servings: 1 serving   **Serving size: One sandwich**

Ingredients
- 1 whole wheat bagel
- 2 tbsps. mustard
- 3 oz. low-sodium deli turkey
- 2 slices of tomatoes
- ¼ avocado (sliced)
- 4 cucumber slices
- ¼ cup baby spinach

Directions Toast the bagel as desired or open the bagel.
Prepare the vegetables as listed above.
Spread the mustard over both sides of the bagel, and then add the ingredients, with the turkey on the bottom.
Serve and enjoy!

Nutritional Information per serving Calories: 433 Fat: 11.5 g Carbohydrates: 53.1/2 g Protein: 30 g

Pork Tenderloin Sandwich

Servings: 1 serving   **Serving size: One sandwich**

Ingredients

For the Sandwich:
- 1 whole wheat hamburger bun
- ½ cup roasted pork tenderloin, sliced.
- 1 tbsp. chimichurri
- 1 tbsp. low fat mayonnaise
- 1 tbsp. sliced onions
- 1 tbsp. sliced apples
- ½ cup sliced tomato
- Arugula for topping, as desired.
- Cooking spray for the skillet pan.

For the Chimichurri:
- 1 cup fresh cilantro
- ¾ cup fresh basil leaves
- ¼ cup white balsamic vinegar
- 2 tbsps. lemon juice
- 2 cloves of garlic
- ½ tbsp. olive oil
- ½ tsp. salt
- ¼ tsp. pepper
- A pinch of red pepper flakes

Directions Preheat a skillet pan to medium high heat.
Prepare the vegetables and fruit as listed above.

Spray the skillet pan with the cooking spray, and add the sliced onion and apples, keeping each on their own side. Sprinkle both sides with the kosher salt and let sit for a couple of minutes to start cooking, listening for the cooking to begin.
Lower the heat to medium-low and cook with covering for 20-30 minutes until caramelized and tender.
Place all the ingredients for the chimichurri in a blender and pulse until fully incorporated. Mix with mayonnaise once ready. Toast the bun as desired and build the sandwich, with the pork on the bottom.
Serve and enjoy!

Nutritional Information per serving Calories: 401 Fat: 1.5 g Carbohydrates: 41.5 g Protein: 34.7 g

Macro Egg Sandwich

Servings: 1 serving   **Serving size: One sandwich**

Ingredients
- Kaiser bun from bakery section
- 1 large egg
- 2 oz. egg whites
- 1 oz. chopped avocado
- 2/3 cups turkey sausage, sliced horizontally to fit on the sandwich
- One slice of reduced fat pepper jack cheese
- ⅛ cups of arugula
- ⅛ cups of red onion slices
- Salt and pepper to taste
- Cooking spray for the skillet pan
- For the sauce:
- 2 tbsps. of light mayonnaise
- ½ minced garlic clove
- 1 tsp. lemon olive oil.

Directions Preheat your skillet to medium.
Prepare the vegetables as listed above.
Mix together the ingredients for the sauce and stir together until fully incorporated.
In a separate bowl, whisk the egg and egg whites and the salt and pepper.
Spray the skillet pan with the cooking spray and add the eggs. Cook for three minutes, or until eggs are almost fully cooked and solid.
Put the cheese over the eggs and remove from heat. Cover it with a lid for two to three minutes to allow the cheese to melt.
Once the cheese is melted, place the eggs on the bottom of the bun. Build with all the other ingredients and enjoy!

Nutritional Information per serving Calories: 365 calories Fat: 17.6 g Carbohydrates: 27.1 g Protein: 24.2 g

Shrimp Cocktail Sub

Servings: 1 serving   **Serving size: One sandwich**

Ingredients
- 4 ciabatta buns, halved
- 1½ lbs. of jumbo 16/20 shrimp, peeled and deveined
- 3 tbsp. olive oil
- 1 tsp. kosher salt
- ½ tsp. black pepper
- 2 cups romaine lettuce chopped, washed and dried
- ¼ cup shaved parmesan cheese
- Macro Caesar Salad Dressing

Directions Set your oven temperature to 400º F.
Prepare the shrimp as mentioned above.
Line a baking sheet with non-stick aluminum foil.
Lay out the shrimp on the baking sheet, and season with olive oil, salt, and pepper.
Bake for 10 minutes while you prepare the Macro Caesar salad dressing.
Toast the buns as desired with the warm oven, and build the sandwich, with the shrimp on the bottom.

Nutritional Information per serving Calories: 659 Fat: 40 g Carbohydrates: 29 g Protein: 43 g

Macro Turkey Club Sandwich

Servings: 1 serving　　　　　　　　　　　　　　　　　　　　　**Serving size:** One sandwich

Ingredients
- 2 slices center cut bacon, cut in half
- 2 slices whole grain bread, thin sliced
- 1 tablespoon light mayo
- 2 slices iceberg lettuce
- 3 oz. deli turkey breast, sliced thin
- 2 slices of a ripe tomato

Directions Preheat a skillet pan to medium heat.
Prepare the vegetables as listed above.
Cook the bacon on the skillet pan to desired crispness.
Allow the bacon to drip dry over a metal rack.
Build the sandwich with the turkey and the bacon on the bottom, and the other ingredients on top.
Serve and enjoy!

Nutritional Information per serving Calories: 351 Fat: 11.5 g Carbohydrates: 28.5 g Protein: 35 g

Hot Sandwiches

Roast Beef Po' Boy

Servings: 8 servings　　　　　　　　　　　　　　　　　　　　　**Serving size:** One sandwich

Ingredients
- 2 ½ - 3 lb. beef chuck shoulder roast
- 1 tablespoon TAK House Seasoning or your favorite beef seasoning
- 4 tablespoons all-purpose flour separated
- ¼ cup canola oil
- 1 yellow onion diced
- 3 cups unsalted or low sodium beef broth
- 1 tsp. Kosher salt
- ½ tsp. black pepper
- Fresh white bakery bread for sandwiches (French loaf, French sticks, or hoagie rolls will do fine)

For the Toppings:
- Tomatoes seeded and sliced ¼ in. thick
- Sliced dill pickles
- Finely shredded Iceberg lettuce
- Mayonnaise

Directions
- Pat the beef roast with a paper towel to dry it, then sprinkle with the listed seasonings along with 2 tbsps. of all-purpose flour. Spread the flour and seasoning all over, evenly coating the roast.
- Pour the oil into a large sauté pan. You can also use a Dutch oven. Set to medium-high heat and allow the oil to get to the proper temperature. Lay the roast on the oiled pan and let it sear for 4 minutes on both sides, or until you see a nice crust. Remove from the pan with tongs and set it to rest on a plate.
- Lower the heat to medium and add the diced onion to the pan. Sauté until the onions are softened, cooking for 3-4 minutes. Add the remaining 2 tbsps. of flour over the onions and stir until fully coated.
- Pour in about half of the beef broth, adding it slowly, stir until completely incorporated. When half of the broth is added, sprinkle in the salt and pepper, then let it simmer until it has thickened.
- Add the beef, along with all of its juices, to your slow cooker. Pour over the sauce, along with the remaining broth. Set your slow cooker on the high heat setting and cover. Cook for 4 hours, then remove the beef and shred it. Add the shredded beef back to the slow cooker and continue to cook (uncovered) for 1½ hours more, stirring occasionally.
- Cut your bread for sandwiches (if necessary). If you'd like to toast your bread, preheat the oven to 400°. Once the oven comes to temperature, place the bread on a baking sheet and bake for 4 minutes or until lightly toasted.

- Remove bread from the oven, slather with mayonnaise (if using), add a generous serving of shredded roast beef and desired toppings.

Nutritional Information per serving Calories: 446 Fat: 27 g Carbohydrates: 14 g Protein: 36 g

Macro French-Dipped Beef Sandwich

Servings: 8 serving   **Serving size: One sandwich**

Ingredients
- 3-4 lbs. chuck roast or rump roast
- salt and pepper to taste
- 1.5 oz. beef broth low sodium
- 10.5 oz. onion soup low sodium
- 1 onion sliced
- 12 oz. light beer
- 2 cloves garlic minced
- 1 sprig rosemary optional
- 1 tsp. Worcestershire sauce
- 8 French rolls (or 2 baguettes cut into 6 in. rolls)
- 8 tablespoons butter

Directions Season the raw roast with salt and pepper. Let the roast brown in a large pan over medium-high heat. Add remaining ingredients but set rolls and butter aside to use later. In a slow cooker, cook on low for 8 hours or on high 4 hours or until beef is tender.
Once the roast is done cooking, remove from the pot, and set it on a plate to rest for 15 minutes. Once the roast has rested, you may shred or slice it.
Spread the butter on the rolls and heat under a broiler until they are lightly toasted. Top rolls with beef and serve with just from the slow cooker for dipping.

Nutritional Information per serving Calories: 741 calories Fat: 34 g Carbohydrates: 63 g Protein: 44 g

Turkey and Spinach Panini

Serving size: 2 servings

Ingredients
- 2 herb and cheese ciabatta bread loaves, sliced
- 4 slices of Havarti cheese
- 4 slices deli turkey (you can also use ham)
- ½ cup fresh spinach leaves
- Light butter or spray butter

Directions Heat skillet to medium-low heat.
Spread the butter over the ciabatta bread or spray with butter.
Add 2 slices turkey (or ham of your choice) 1 slice of Havarti cheese, spinach leaves in between each bread slice.
Cook until cheese is melted and bread is toasted, flip frequently.

Macro Philly Cheese Steak

Servings: 4 servings   **Serving size: One sandwich**

Ingredients
- 1 lb. lean ground beef
- 1½ cups fresh bell peppers
- 1½ cups onions
- ½ tsp. salt to taste
- ½ tsp. black pepper to taste
- ½ tsp. chili powder to taste
- ½ tsp. paprika to taste
- 1 tsp. Italian seasoning
- 1 tbsp. olive oil
- 4 hamburger buns
- 4 thin provolone cheese slices

Directions Preheat a skillet pan to medium heat.

Chop the onions and peppers into small pieces for the sandwich.
Cook the ground beef and the peppers together, stirring to cook the meat evenly.
When the meat has browned, add the desired spices and stir to incorporate.
Melt the cheese on top of the meat.
Toast the hamburger buns to desired extent and serve meat into buns. Enjoy!

Nutritional Information per serving Calories: 232 Fat: 12 g Carbohydrates: 5 g Protein: 27 g

Shrimp Po' Boy

Servings: 2 servings

Ingredients

For the sauce
- 1 cup Greek yogurt
- 2 tbsps. of Dijon mustard
- 2 cloves of minced garlic
- 1 tsp. of Cajun seasoning
- ½ tsp. hot sauce
- 1 tsp. Worcestershire sauce
- 1 tbsp. olive oil

Sandwich toppings
- 1 lb. of shrimp
- 1 tsp. paprika
- ¼ tsp. cayenne
- Salt and pepper to taste
- 4 rolls of white bread of your choice
- Sliced tomatoes
- Shredded lettuce

Directions Mix Greek yogurt, Dijon mustard, garlic, Cajun seasoning, hot sauce, and Worcestershire sauce in a small bowl until fully incorporated.
Heat a large sauté pan over medium-high, add olive oil and garlic and cook 1-2 minutes. Add in shrimp and sprinkle with paprika, cayenne, salt, and pepper. Cook the shrimp for 5-6 minutes, or until it is no longer pink. Remove from the saucepan to rest.
Cut the bread in half lengthwise and add a generous spread of remoulade sauce. Pile with shrimp, lettuce, and tomato. Serve and enjoy!

Miami Cuban Sandwich

Servings: 1 serving

Ingredients
- 1 roll Cuban bread
- 4 slices sweet ham
- 3 slices slow roasted pork
- 5 slices Swiss cheese
- Yellow mustard
- Dill pickle for sandwiches
- Butter for cooking

Directions Cut off the ends of the Cuban bread, then slice in half.
Add mustard, then ham, then pork, then cheese, then pickles, then place the bun on top.
Place the sandwich on a pan or griddle over low heat, then brush top with melted butter.
Press the sandwich with a panini press, or if you don't have a press use a heavy pot or pie dish and push down.
Cook 5-10 minutes on each side or until golden brown and cheese is melted and enjoy!

Nutritional Information per serving Calories: 213 Fat: 28 g Carbohydrates: 15.6 g Protein: 80 g

Medianoche (Midnight) Cuban Sandwich

Servings: 4 servings

Serving size: One sandwich

Ingredients
- 4 sweet bread rolls
- ½ cups mayonnaise
- ¼ cups prepared mustard
- 1 lb. thinly sliced cooked ham
- 1 lb. thinly sliced fully cooked pork
- 1 lb. sliced Swiss cheese
- 1 cup dill pickle slices
- 2 tbsps. butter, melted

Directions Split the sandwich rolls in half and spread mustard and mayonnaise liberally onto the cut sides.
On each sandwich, place an equal amount of Swiss cheese, ham, and pork in exactly that order.
Place a few pickles onto each one and put the top of the roll onto the sandwich.
Brush the tops with melted butter.
Press each sandwich in a sandwich press heated to medium-high heat. If a sandwich press is not available, use a large skillet over medium-high heat, and press the sandwiches down using a sturdy plate or skillet. Some indoor grills may be good for this also.
Cook for 5 to 8 minutes, keeping sandwiches pressed. If using a skillet, you may want to flip them once for even browning.
Slice diagonally and serve hot and enjoy!

Nutritional Information per serving Calories: 453 Fat: 88.4 g Carbohydrates: 69.1 g Protein: 91 g

Breakfast sandwich

Servings: 4 servings

Serving size: One sandwich

Ingredients
- 4 whole wheat muffins
- 6 medium eggs
- ¼ cup of nonfat milk
- 12 slices smoked deli turkey
- ¼ cup of shredded low-fat cheddar cheese
- Salt and pepper to taste
- Cooking spray for baking

Directions Preheat the oven to 350º F.
Spray a baking pan large enough for the eggs with the cooking spray.
Mix the eggs, milk, salt, and pepper in a small bowl and whisk until fully incorporated. Pour into the prepared baking pan.
Bake for 12-14 minutes or until the eggs are set. Remove the eggs from the oven and let them cool to room temperature. Cut the eggs into four squares, as evenly as possible.
Assemble with the eggs on the bottom and the turkey right above.
Add the shredded cheddar above them and toast until muffins are crispy and the cheese is melted.

Nutritional Information per serving Calories: 331 Fat: 12.5 g Carbohydrates: 25.5 g Protein: 29 g

Turkey Meatball Sub

Servings: 8 servings

Serving size: One sandwich

Ingredients
- 1 lb. of lean ground turkey
- ½ cups Panko breadcrumbs
- ¼ cups shredded Parmesan cheese
- 1 large egg
- 4 cloves of garlic, minced
- 1 tbsp. of dried oregano
- ½ tbsp. of dried basil
- 1 tbsp. of fresh chopped parsley
- 1 tbsp. of ground onion powder
- ½ tbsp. of sea salt
- 2 tsps. of black pepper
- 24 oz. of canned diced tomatoes
- 8 whole wheat hot dog buns
- 8 slices of reduced fat provolone cheese
- Fresh shredded basil (optional)

Directions
- Set the oven to 350º F. Make sure the oven racks are on top, measuring at about 1/3 of the oven. Line two baking sheets with parchment paper or foil that's been coated with nonfat cooking spray.
- Combine turkey, breadcrumbs, parmesan cheese, egg, oregano, parsley, basil, garlic and salt and pepper into a large bowl. Shape the turkey mixture into small meatballs. Once formed, place the meatballs on the greased baking sheet; the recipe should yield about 32 tablespoon-sized meatballs,
- Bake in the oven for around 10 to 15 minutes, checking the temperature and color of the meatballs and shaking every 5 minutes.
- While the meatballs cook, grab a small saucepan and heat up the can of diced tomatoes. You can add in additional seasonings like garlic, parsley, oregano, basil, salt and pepper for extra flavor if the can does not include them.
- Remove the meatballs from the oven when they have finished cooking, removing the meatballs from the pans. Place rolls on the same baking sheets; top each piece with 4 meatballs. Spoon about 3 tablespoons sauce over meatballs in each sandwich; top each with 1 slice of light provolone cheese. Bake until cheese is melted and sandwiches are heated through, about 5 to 7 minutes.

Nutritional Information per serving Calories: 271 Fat: 9.9 g Carbohydrates: 24.5 g Protein: 23.7 g

Open-Faced Spinach and Cheese Melt

Servings: 4 servings **Serving size: One sandwich**

Ingredients
- 10-oz. pkg frozen spinach thawed
- Kosher salt and pepper
- 1½ cups Comte or fontina cheese grated
- Half of a French baguette or loaf

Directions
- Heat your broiler with the rack 4 to 6 in. from the element.
- Thaw spinach, then squeeze out water making sure the spinach is dry. You can also use a colander to press out the water.
- Sprinkle the dry spinach into a medium sized bowl and season with some salt and pepper, then mix in with cheese.
- Split a French baguette or loaf in half, lengthwise. Toast baguette halves under a broiler until crisp at the top but not brown.
- Spread the spinach and cheese mixture evenly over the toasted halves. Add them back into the broiler until melted for 3 to 5 minutes.
- Cut in half, serve hot, and enjoy!

Nutritional Information per serving Calories: 504 Fat: 21 g Carbohydrates: 49 g Protein: 44 g

Turkey Reuben Sandwich

Servings: 4 servings **Serving size: One sandwich**

Ingredients
- 2 tbsp. light mayonnaise
- 2 slices (1 oz) Swiss cheese
- ½ cup sauerkraut
- 8 oz. sliced deli turkey
- 4 slices regular Rye Bread
- 2 tbsps. olive oil
- 4 tsps. pepper

Directions
- Preheat a skillet with the olive oil to medium-high heat or your oven to 350 degrees F.
- Take two pieces of rye bread and spread the light mayonnaise on one side of each.

- On the skillet, lay down the slices of rye with the mayo sides facing up, let them lightly toast, for about 3 minutes, then remove and set aside. For the oven, let the slices toast on a baking sheet with oil or parchment paper for 5 minutes.
- Once the pieces of the bread are lightly toasted, go ahead and make your sandwich, adding the turkey, sauerkraut, Swiss cheese, and pepper to taste.
- In the skillet, add the sandwich back and cook until the cheese is melted. In the oven, cook for another 5 minutes.
- Serve hot and enjoy!

Wraps

Vegan Bean Burrito

Servings: 4 servings **Serving size: One burrito**

Ingredients

For the beans:
- ½ cup dried black beans, or 1 can drained and rinsed
- 1 tsp. olive oil
- ½ cup onion, chopped
- 2 cloves garlic, minced
- 1 small Roma tomato, chopped
- ¼ tsp. cumin
- ¼ tsp. dried oregano
- ¼ tsp. salt
- ¼ cup water

For the burrito:
- 4 large whole wheat tortillas
- ½ cup cooked brown rice
- ½ cup salsa
- ½ cup guacamole, or 1 avocado sliced
- 1 cup cherry tomatoes, halved
- ¼ cup romaine lettuce, shredded

Directions
- Soak the beans overnight in water if they are dried. Otherwise, drain the fluid from the can.
- Place the beans in a sauce pot with four cups of water and bring to a boil.
- Lower heat to a simmer and let the beans cook for 45 minutes.
- When the beans are almost done, preheat the skillet to medium heat.
- Add oil to the skillet and cook the onions until they're translucent.
- Add the tomatoes, garlic, cumin, oregano, and sea salt to the skillet, and cook while stirring for one minute.
- Add the beans to the mix and bring the pan to a boil. Then lower the heat and simmer for ten minutes.
- Remove the skillet from heat and allow it to cool for ten minutes.
- Mash the beans to thicken.
- Toast the tortillas on a fresh skillet pan for one to two minutes on each side if desired.
- Separate each ingredient to four equal portions and wrap the beans and chopped vegetables in the tortillas.
- Serve and enjoy!

Nutritional Information per serving Calories: 208 Fat: 3 g Carbohydrates: 40 g Protein: 7 g

Vegan Chickpea Gyro

Servings: 4 servings **Serving size: One gyro**

Ingredients
- 1½ cups of chickpeas
- 1 tbsp. olive oil
- 1 tbsp. paprika
- 1 tsp. ground black pepper
- ½ tsp. cayenne pepper
- ¼ tsp. salt
- 4 pita flatbreads
- 1 cup macro basil vinaigrette
- ¼ red onion cut into strips
- 2 lettuce leaves roughly chopped
- 1 tomato sliced

Directions Preheat the oven to 400º F.
Dry the chickpeas with a paper towel, removing any skins that come off.
Mix the chickpeas in a bowl with the oil and spices.
Spread the chickpeas across a cooking tray with aluminum foil and bake for 20 minutes.
As the chickpeas bake, chop the vegetables and separate them into four equal portions.
When the chickpeas are ready, put them on the pita and wrap with ingredients.
Drizzle dressing on top of one hole of the gyro or before wrapping.
Serve and enjoy!

Nutritional Information per serving Calories: 208 Fat: 12.6 g Carbohydrates: 45 g Protein: 11.5 g

Spicy Chicken Burrito

Servings: 8 servings   **Serving size: One burrito**

Ingredients
- One cup of cooked brown rice
- ⅛ tsp. salt
- 2 cups shredded cooked chicken breast
- 15 oz. black beans, drained, rinsed
- 1 cup mild salsa
- 2 tsps. chili powder
- ¼ cup chopped fresh cilantro
- 1 tablespoon lime juice
- 8 low-fat whole wheat tortillas (8-in.)
- 1 cup shredded reduced fat sharp cheddar cheese

Directions
- Mix the chicken, black beans, salsa and chili powder in a bowl, and microwave it on high for two minutes, or until hot, and stir it.
- Stir in the cooked rice, the cilantro, and the lime juice.
- Toast the tortillas in a skillet pan for one to two minutes on both sides and then serve the fillings in eight different tortillas. Enjoy!

Nutritional Information per serving Calories: 240 Fat: 8 g Carbohydrates: 23 g Protein: 18 g

Beef Burrito

Servings: 4 servings

Ingredients
- 1 lb. lean ground beef, minced
- 1 tbsp. of Coconut oil
- ½ can chopped tomatoes
- ½ finely chopped red & yellow pepper
- ½ finely chopped red onion
- 1 tsp. garlic powder.
- ¾ cups egg whites
- 1 tsp. each of paprika, chili powder, crushed chili flakes, garlic powder, dried oregano
- Salt and pepper to taste
- Handful of fresh coriander
- Salsa of your choice for topping

Directions
- Preheat your grill to 400º F. Cook your ground beef in a frying pan with coconut oil until the meat is browned. Set aside in a bowl.
- Add the pepper, onions and garlic to the pan and fry them until softened. Then add your meat back to the pan along with the diced tomatoes and seasonings.
- Turn the heat down to low and leave it to simmer for about 10 minutes.
- Heat another large frying pan with coconut oil and pour in your liquid egg whites.
- Once the egg whites have set on the bottom, transfer the pan to the grill and leave for 5-10 minutes until the egg whites are slightly crisp.

- Place your egg white tortilla on a flat baking tray lined with parchment paper. Next, add your spicy beef burrito mixture to the tortilla and sprinkle over some fresh coriander leaves. Then fold up the wrap into a burrito shape.
- Spread your tomato salsa all over the top of the burrito, as desired, and then grate over your cheese until the top is covered. You may sprinkle over some more crushed chilies if you like, and then place it into the oven. Bake for 10-15 minutes until the cheese has melted and turns golden brown and crisp.
- Serve hot and enjoy!

Nutritional Information per serving Calories: 240 Fat: 8 g Carbohydrates: 23 g Protein: 18 g

Chipotle Turkey Wrap

Servings: 4 servings   **Serving size: One Wrap**

Ingredients
- ½ cup mayonnaise
- 1 tbsp. chipotle chili in Adobo sauce
- 2 tsps. Adobo sauce from chipotle peppers
- 4 (10 in.) whole wheat tortillas
- ½ lb. sliced smoked turkey
- 8 oz. shredded Monterey Jack cheese
- 1 avocado
- 4 romaine lettuce leaves

Directions Peel and pit the avocado.
Chop the romaine lettuce leaves coarsely.
Dice the chipotle peppers and the avocado.
Form with all ingredients in the wraps evenly.
Serve and enjoy!

Nutritional Information per serving Calories: 729 Fat: 52.4 g Carbohydrates: 57.3 g Protein: 23.3 g

Portobello Mushroom Gyros

Servings: 4 servings   **Serving size: One Wrap**

Ingredients
- 4 portobello mushrooms
- ¼ cup olive oil
- 2 tbsps. soy sauce
- 2 tbsps. lemon juice
- 4 cloves garlic minced
- ½ tsp. each oregano, smoked paprika, salt, pepper
- 4 large pita breads
- ¼ cup macro basil vinaigrette
- Optional toppings: Lettuce, tomato, red onion, feta cheese

Directions Preheat a skillet pan to medium heat.
Cut the stems from the mushrooms and clean under cold water.
Cut the mushrooms into ¼-in. slices, cleaning again if excess dirt is found.
Mix the oil, soy, lemon, garlic, and spices in a small bowl until incorporated.
Mix the mushrooms in the bowl until marinated with the sauce.
Cook the mushrooms for about 5 minutes, flipping to evenly cook. The goal is a deep brown color and slight softness.
Separate the ingredients into four equal servings and wrap them into the gyros.
Serve and enjoy!

Nutritional Information per serving Calories: 386 Fat: 21.5 g Carbohydrates: 40.6 g Protein: 9.3 g

Breakfast Wrap

Servings: 4 servings   **Serving size: One Wrap**

Ingredients

- 8 large eggs
- ½ tbsp. milk
- 1 tbsp. olive oil
- 1 tbsp. minced garlic
- 1 medium red pepper, finely minced
- ½ medium red onion, finely minced
- 4 pieces of thick-cut bacon, cooked until crispy
- Salt and pepper, to taste
- 4 Multigrain flatbreads

Directions Preheat a skillet pan to medium heat.
Mince the red peppers, tomatoes, and onions.
Crack all the eggs in a large bowl and add the milk. Scramble until fully mixed.
Cook the bacon to desired crispness on a skillet pan, and let drip dry on a net tray.
While cooking the bacon, preheat another skillet at medium heat.
When the bacon is done, add the olive oil to the skillet and cook the vegetables until the onions are translucent.
Remove the vegetables from the skillet and add more oil if needed to cook the eggs.
Cook the eggs until they lose all liquid.
Separate all the ingredients into four separate servings and wrap into the flatbreads. Enjoy!

Nutritional Information per serving Calories: 355 Fat: 24.5 g Carbohydrates: 10.4 g Protein: 23.3 g

Chicken Gyro

Servings: 8 servings   **Serving size: One gyro**

Ingredients

- 2 lbs. chicken tenderloins
- 1½ tbsps. olive oil
- 1 tbsp. freshly squeezed lemon juice
- 3 cloves garlic, minced
- 2 tsps. dried oregano
- 1 tsp. dried thyme
- ½ tsp. paprika
- Kosher salt and freshly ground black pepper, to taste
- 8 pita flatbreads
- 2 cups shredded romaine
- 2 cups cherry tomatoes, quartered
- 1 red onion, thinly sliced
- Top with Macro Basil Vinaigrette if desired

Directions In a gallon size plastic bag, combine the chicken, olive oil, lemon juice, garlic, oregano, thyme, paprika, 1 tsp. salt and 1/2 tsp. pepper.
Allow the bag to marinate for at least two hours, turning occasionally to fully incorporate all the juices, draining out the excess fluids.
Preheat a grill to medium heat, and add the chicken, cooking on each side for four minutes or until internal temperature reaches 165 degrees.
Mince the vegetables while allowing the chicken to rest.
Cut the chicken into small pieces.
Separate the ingredients to four equal portions. Add all the ingredients to the wraps, and fold.
Serve and enjoy!

Nutritional Information (Without Vinaigrette) per serving Calories: 298 Fat: 6.1/2 g Carbohydrates: 30.2 g Protein: 29.7 g

Spicy Shrimp Wrap

Servings: 6 servings   **Serving size: One wrap**

Ingredients

- 1 cup fresh salsa of your choice
- 1 medium ripe mango, peeled, pitted and diced
- 1 tbsp. ketchup
- 1 tbsp. taco seasoning
- 1 tbsp. olive oil
- 1 lb. uncooked medium shrimp, peeled and deveined
- 6 10-in. whole wheat flour tortillas, warmed
- ½ cup coleslaw mix
- 6 tablespoons reduced fat sour cream

Directions Preheat a skillet pan to medium-high heat.
Combine the ketchup, salsa, and mango in a bowl.
Put the taco seasoning, oil, and shrimp in a plastic bag and shake.
Cook the shrimp for two to three minutes on the skillet or until pink.
Separate the ingredients into six equal parts.
Form the wrap and top with sour cream as desired and enjoy!

Nutritional Information per serving Calories: 374 Fat: 9 g Carbohydrates: 46 g Protein: 20 g

Tuna Salad Wrap

Servings: One serving

Ingredients
- 10-in. soft flour tortilla
- 5oz. can chunk light tuna fish, in water, drained
- ¼ cup plain Greek yogurt
- 1 tsp. Dijon mustard
- 2 tbsps. chopped walnuts
- 2 tbsps. raisins
- 1 tbsp. capers
- 1 tbsp. chopped flat parsley
- A pinch salt and pepper
- ½ cup baby spinach leaves (or other leafy greens)

Directions Using a fork, combine the tuna, yogurt, Dijon mustard, chopped walnuts, raisins, capers, parsley, salt, and pepper in a mixing bowl.
Put spinach leaves in the center of the tortilla.
Dump the tuna fish salad right on top of the spinach.
Fold the wrap tightly and enjoy!

Nutritional Information per serving Calories: 481 Fat: 41 g Carbohydrates: 45 g Protein: 29.7 g

Beef Gyro

Servings: 8 servings   Serving size: One gyro

Ingredients
- 2 lbs. beef tenderloin
- 1½ tbsps. olive oil
- 1 tbsp. freshly squeezed lemon juice
- 3 cloves garlic, minced
- 2 tsps. dried oregano
- 1 tsp. dried thyme
- ½ tsp. paprika
- Kosher salt and freshly ground black pepper, to taste
- 8 pita flatbreads
- 2 cups shredded romaine
- 2 cups cherry tomatoes, quartered
- 1 red onion, thinly sliced
- Top with Macro Basil Vinaigrette, if desired

Directions In a gallon size plastic bag, combine the beef, olive oil, lemon juice, garlic, oregano, thyme, paprika, 1 tsp. salt and 1/2 tsp. pepper.
Allow the bag to marinate for at least two hours, turning occasionally to fully incorporate all the juices, draining out the excess fluids.
Preheat a grill to medium heat and cut the beef tenderloins into 2-in. fillets.
Cook the beef, cooking on each side for 1-2 minutes or until medium-rare (You can choose your own level of cooking, but this is recommended). Mince the vegetables.
Separate the ingredients to four equal portions. Add all the ingredients to the wraps, and fold.
Serve and enjoy!

Nutritional Information (Without Vinaigrette) per serving Calories: 883 Fat: 28 g   Carbohydrates: 38.9 g Protein: 29.7 g

Lamb Gyro

Servings: 8 servings **Serving size: One gyro**

Ingredients
- 2 lbs. ground lamb tenderloins
- 1½ tbsps. olive oil
- 1 tbsp. freshly squeezed lemon juice
- 3 cloves garlic, minced
- 2 tsps. dried oregano
- 1 tsp. dried thyme
- ½ tsp. paprika
- Kosher salt and freshly ground black pepper, to taste
- 8 pita flatbreads
- 2 cups shredded romaine
- 2 cups cherry tomatoes, quartered
- 1 red onion, thinly sliced
- Top with Macro Basil Vinaigrette, if desired.

Directions In a gallon size plastic bag, combine the lamb, olive oil, lemon juice, garlic, oregano, thyme, paprika, 1 tsp. salt and 1/2 tsp. pepper.
Allow the bag to marinate for at least two hours, turning occasionally to fully incorporate all the juices, draining out the excess fluids.
Preheat a grill to medium heat and cut the lamb tenderloins into 2-in. fillets.
Cook the lamb on each side for 1-2 minutes or until medium-rare (you can choose your own level of cooking, but this is recommended).
Mince the vegetables.
Separate the ingredients to four equal portions.
Add all the ingredients to the wraps, and fold.
Serve and enjoy!

Nutritional Information (Without Vinaigrette) per serving Calories: 937 Fat: 40 g Carbohydrates: 38.9 g Protein: 98.1 g

Chapter 5: Poultry

The Chicken and the Turkey

Poultry products are great for just about any type of dish. Whole roasted chicken or oven-baked turkeys are among the first dishes that come to mind for people when thinking of poultry dishes. While those recipes are fantastic on their own, poultry has another added benefit. It is the animal protein with the least amount of saturated fats, discounting seafood, and carries a high amount of protein in every dish. It's also the most affordable protein, which makes it perfect for your wallet and your health.

Poultry products can spread many foodborne illnesses. It is best to take every precaution when storing raw poultry and leftovers and thoroughly cook the poultry to an acceptable temperature to prevent salmonella and food poisoning. It's also vital to debone chickens and turkeys properly to avoid getting any bones stuck in your digestive system, which can lead to severe health complications. As always, it's best to not overstock your kitchen and cook every raw ingredient within its proper shelf life to avoid foodborne illnesses and to be careful in food preparation.

Otherwise, poultry dishes are filling, delicious, and perfect for the macro diet. The focus on chickens and turkeys is due to their accessibility to most people. Poultry such as ducks, quails, and other commonly eaten poultry sources won't appear here. That doesn't discredit their worth as replacements for your diet if you can afford them or eat them regularly so long as you maintain the balance demanded by the diet. With that said, see what this chapter has to offer you and your pursuit of the Macro diet.

Shopping List

- Chicken
- Smoked chicken sausage
- Chicken katsu
- Eggs
- Bacon
- Ground turkey
- Andouille sausage
- Turkey legs
- Rice
- Basmati rice
- Hamburger buns
- All-purpose flour
- Lo-Dough
- Corn flakes
- Corn starch
- Pie crust
- Evaporated cane sugar
- Brown sugar
- Vegetable oil
- Olive oil
- Cooking oil
- Rice vinegar
- White wine
- Sake
- Dashi
- Mirin
- Carrot
- Peas
- Tomato

- Polenta
- Onion
- Yellow onion
- Celery
- Red bell peppers
- Green bell peppers
- Russet potatoes
- Cauliflower
- Jalapeno pepper
- Corn
- Pearl onion
- Sweet potato
- Lettuce
- Zucchini
- Yellow squash
- Mushrooms
- Okra
- Scallions
- Black beans
- Orange
- Lemon
- lime
- Unsweetened almond milk
- Milk
- Half and half
- Butter
- Sour cream
- Mozzarella sticks
- Feta cheese
- Garlic

- Garlic powder
- Onion powder
- Bay leaves
- Parsley
- Thyme
- Oregano
- Fresh ginger
- Allspice
- Cinnamon
- Coriander
- File powder
- Creole seasoning
- Cumin
- Paprika
- Caraway seeds
- Curry powder
- Chili powder
- Salt
- Pepper
- Tomato paste
- Mayflower curry sauce
- Worcestershire sauce
- Salsa verde
- Chicken stock
- Hot sauce
- Mayonnaise
- Soy sauce
- Hoisin sauce

Stews

Tochitura de Pui (Romanian Chicken Stew)

Servings: 4 servings   **Serving size:** ¼ of the dish

Ingredients
- A 1.1 lbs. pork neck
- 1 tbsp. of lard or 2 tbsps. vegetable oil
- 1 large onion
- 4 small coarsely-ground smoked chicken sausages
- 3 garlic cloves, whole
- 2 tbsps. of tomato paste
- 2 bay leaves
- 1 cup dry white wine
- 4 eggs
- 2-3 tbsps. of vegetable oil
- ½ cup of feta cheese (sheep's cheese is better)
- Fresh parsley to garnish
- Polenta and pickled vegetables for serving

Directions
- Start by chopping up the meat into small cubes. Pat them dry with a paper towel.
- Let the lard melt in the cast-iron pan or grease with oil. Evenly brown the meat in two batches if your pan is not large enough.
- Return the meat to the pan, then add finely chopped onions and 1/2 tsp. salt.
- Add ¼ cup water and cover, letting it cook for about 20 minutes or until the meat is tender. Add more water if the dish is becoming too dry.
- Start cooking the polenta.
- Cut the sausages into slices, about 0.4 in.es thick. Mince garlic.
- Add the sausages, garlic, tomato paste and bay leaves to the pan.
- Pour the white wine, cover it, then continue cooking for 10 minutes until the meat is tender. Make sure the sausages are cooked all the way through.
- Adjust the taste with salt and pepper.
- While the meat cooks, heat a frying pan with vegetable oil and fry the eggs.
- Divide the stew between four serving dishes, place a fried egg on top of each dish, then crumble some of the feta (or sheep cheese) on top of each plate.
- Sprinkle some parsley over the dish.
- Serve hot with the polenta and pickled vegetables and enjoy!

Nutritional Information per serving Calories: 808 Fat: 0 g Carbohydrates: 9 g Protein: 52 g

Chicken Goulash

Servings: 6 servings

Ingredients
- 2 tablespoons olive oil
- 2 medium onions sliced
- 1 green bell pepper sliced
- 1 red bell pepper sliced
- 1 cup of smoked lardons or chopped bacon
- 4 tsps. smoked paprika
- 1 tsp. caraway seeds
- 3 cloves garlic crushed or grated
- 2 lbs. chicken thigh cut into bite-size pieces
- 14 oz. can of diced tomatoes
- Salt and pepper to taste
- For serving:
- Rice, pasta, mash or baked potatoes, or bread
- Sour cream (optional)
- 2 tbsps. parsley

Directions
- Add the onions, peppers, and olive oil to a large saucepan, then fry over medium heat for 5 minutes. Cook until the onions and peppers are softened but not brown.
- Add the chopped bacon (or lardons) and turn up the heat to medium-high. Fry the lardons, peppers, and onions for 3 minutes or until lightly browned.
- Reduce the heat to medium and add the paprika, caraway seeds and garlic, then fry for 1 minute.

- Add in the chicken, canned tomatoes, salt, and pepper to taste, then bring to a boil.
- Turn heat to medium-low, cover, and let it simmer for 45 minutes. Add up to ¼ cup of water if it gets too dry. You can also cook this stew in the oven. Cook at 350º F for the same length of time, or longer.
- Serve with rice (pasta, potatoes, or bread), sour cream, and a sprinkling of parsley, and enjoy!

Nutritional Information per serving Calories: 449 Fat: 33 g Carbohydrates: 12 g Protein: 25 g

Japanese Chicken Curry

Servings: 1 serving

Ingredients
- Half a piece of Lo-Dough, crush into crumbs
- 1 chicken breast with the skin removed
- 1 small egg, beaten (for egg-wash)
- 1 tsp. of curry powder
- ½ cups of Mayflower curry sauce
- ¾ cups of cooked basmati rice
- Cooking oil
- Salt and pepper to taste

Directions
- Preheat your oven 400º F.
- Season the chicken with salt and pepper then add it to the bowl with the beaten egg and coat evenly.
- Add the curry powder to the Lo-Dough crumbs and mix in a separate bowl. Add the egg-coated chicken to the crumb mixture and evenly coat. Press the crumbs onto the chicken with your hands to create a thicker crust.
- Spray each piece of chicken with a few sprays of cooking spray and put on a tray and into the oven. Halfway through the cooking time, you can give them a few more sprays to help it crisp up. Let the chicken cook for 15-20 minutes.
- While the chicken is cooking, follow instructions to prepare your curry sauce and cook your rice.
- Take the chicken out of the oven and allow it to rest on a cold plate for a couple of minutes. Slice into bite-sized pieces.
- Serve with rice and sauce, then enjoy!

Nutritional Information per serving Calories: 466 Fat: 15 g Carbohydrates: 47 g Protein: 33 g

Chicken and Black Bean Stew

Servings: 4 servings

Ingredients
- 12 oz. boneless, skinless, chicken breast
- 1 tsp. black pepper
- 1 tsp. garlic powder
- 1 tbsp. extra virgin olive oil
- ½ yellow onion, diced
- 1 Jalapeno, diced
- 3 cloves fresh garlic, diced
- 1 15 oz. can black beans
- ¼ cup cherry tomatoes, diced
- 1 tsp. reduced sodium chicken base
- 1 tbsp salsa verde (optional)

Directions
- Heat a deep stovetop pan with a lid to medium heat, while the pan is heating season the chicken breast on both sides, with black pepper and garlic powder. Once the pan is hot, add 1 tbsp. oil to the pan.
- Place the chicken immediately in the pan, leave it there on medium heat for 2 minutes, then flip to the other side and cook for an additional 2 minutes.
- Both sides should start to become golden brown, but the center will still look uncooked. If not, give each side another minute…your pan wasn't hot enough. Then reduce heat to low and cover the chicken with a lid. Let it cook for about 6 minutes, then flip and cover again for another 6 minutes on the other side. This is based on 2, 6 oz. breasts. If using another size breast, cook 1 minute per oz per side covered.

- After 6 minutes on each side covered, the chicken should be done. But this does depend on the size of the chicken breast...again these times are based on a 6 oz. breast.
- It is recommended to check the internal temperature of the chicken before serving.
- Once the chicken is done remove the chicken from the pan, saving the juices from the chicken in the pan. Allow the chicken to rest while you cook the remaining ingredients.
- Leaving the pan on the stove at medium heat, add the diced onion, jalapeno, and garlic to the pan with the chicken juices. Cook down for 3-5 minutes until most of the liquid has been absorbed.
- Now add your black beans, chicken stock paste, and water (or 1 cup chicken stock) to the pan and cook for about 4 minutes on medium heat, just enough to get the chicken stock to start boiling. Then turn the heat down to medium-low, add your cherry tomatoes, and cook for another 4 minutes.
- While the beans are cooking, shred your chicken breast using a knife and fork.
- Plate by spooning your black beans and broth into your serving bowl. Then top with your shredded chicken, and if you have salsa verde, top your chicken with salsa. The salsa adds a nice, sweet flavor and rounds out the spice in the dish.

Nutritional Information per serving Calories: 228 Fat: 6.2 g Carbohydrates: 21.6 g Protein: 24.9 g

Leftover Thanksgiving Turkey Stew

Servings: 4 servings   **Serving size: 1 1/4 cups**

Ingredients
- 2 tablespoons butter (ghee or coconut oil may be substituted)
- 2 ribs celery sliced
- 2 oz. yellow onion chopped
- ¼ cups carrot diced
- ½ tsps. dried thyme
- ¼ tsp. black pepper freshly ground
- 1 tsp. onion powder
- 4 cups chicken stock (32 oz.) packaged broth or stock works fine as well.
- 1 lb. cooked chicken or turkey meat (about 2 cups) cut or torn into bite-sized chunks
- sea salt to taste
- 1 tbsp. fresh parsley chopped

Directions
- Heat a large soup pot to medium-high heat and add butter. You may also use a Dutch oven. When the butter has melted, add the sliced celery, chopped onion, and diced carrots.
- Stir the celery, onion, and carrots occasionally until they are just beginning to soften but have no color. Add in the thyme and black pepper. Continue to cook vegetables until they are crisp-tender.
- Add the onion powder and broth, stirring as they are added. Add in the chicken or leftover turkey meat.
- Once the meat has been added, bring the soup to a simmer. Let it simmer, until vegetables are tender, stirring occasionally.
- Add salt to taste. You may not need to add any if your broth is not low sodium. If you did use low-sodium broth, you may need to add ½-1 tsp. of salt.
- Sprinkle with parsley before serving and enjoy!

Venezuelan Chupe (Chicken Stew)

Servings: 6 servings

Ingredients
- ¼ cup butter
- 1 large onion, chopped
- 3 russet potatoes, peeled and diced
- 3 skinless, boneless chicken breast halves, diced
- 8 cups water
- 2 cups frozen corn
- Salt to taste
- Ground black pepper to taste
- ½ cup milk, or to taste
- 4 (1 oz.) pieces mozzarella cheese sticks, coarsely chopped

Directions

- In a large pot over medium heat, melt your butter. Once the butter has melted, add your potatoes and chopped onion. Stir the veggies constantly, until soft but not brown, this will take about 5 minutes. Once the potatoes and onions are soft, increase heat to medium-high and add the chicken.
- Cook until the chicken is white, this will take around 7 to 10 minutes. Add water and bring to a simmer, then add corn and bring the soup to a simmer.
- Season soup with salt and pepper to taste, then add the milk and mozzarella cheese.
- Serve hot and enjoy!

Nutritional Information per serving Calories: 362 Fat: 13.1 g Carbohydrates: 40.9 g Protein: 22.6 g

Japanese Turkey Curry

Servings: 6 servings

Ingredients
- 1 lbs. lean ground turkey
- 3 tbsp olive oil
- 1 cup red onion, diced
- 2 potatoes, russet, or golden
- ½ head cauliflower
- 2 cloves garlic, pressed
- 1 tbsp. fresh ginger, peeled and grated or minced
- 1 cup reduced sodium chicken stock
- 1 tbsp. Mirin, Shaoxing wine, or dry sherry
- 2 tbsp. curry powder

Directions
- In a large saucepan, sauté onion in olive oil over low heat until translucent.
- Add meat to pan and cook until browned, flipping and chopping to make crumbles.
- Add garlic and ginger, sauté for 2 minutes.
- Add dry spices and mix thoroughly to coat meat.
- Add potatoes, chicken stock and cooking wine. Bring to a low boil and simmer for 30 minutes.
- Add cauliflower and any other vegetables, simmer for 20-30 minutes until done adding water as needed.
- Serve with rice and enjoy!

Nutritional Information per serving Calories: 262 Fat: 12 g Carbohydrates: 20 g Protein: 18 g

Buffalo Chicken Stew

Servings: 2 servings

Ingredients
- 2 tablespoons of olive oil
- 1 onion, diced
- 1 carrot, sliced
- 2 garlic cloves, sliced
- A quarter of celery root, diced
- 1 red bell pepper, sliced
- 10 oz. of chicken breast, cubed
- sea salt
- pepper
- 3 cups of chicken stock
- ⅓ cup hot sauce

Directions Heat the olive oil in a large pot and add the onion, carrot, garlic, celery, and bell peppers. Cook until soft.
Add the chicken, season with sea salt and pepper, then cook and stir until the chicken turns opaque-white.
Add the chicken stock and hot sauce and bring to a boil.
Reduce to a simmer and cook on low heat for 30 minutes, until the chicken pieces are cooked through.
Serve and enjoy!

Nutritional Information per serving Calories: 559 Fat: 32 g Carbohydrates: 27 g Protein: 41 g

Chicken Noodle Stew

Servings: 10 servings **Serving size: 1¼ cups**

Ingredients
- 1 tbsp. unsalted butter
- ¾ cup chopped yellow onion (1/2 of a medium onion)
- 1 cup sliced carrots (1 and 1/2 large carrots)
- 1 cup sliced celery (2–3 stalks)
- 2 garlic cloves, minced
- ¼ cup all-purpose flour
- ½ tsp. oregano
- ½ tsp. fresh ground black pepper
- 1 tsp. fresh thyme
- ½ tsp. salt
- 8 cups chicken broth
- 1 medium potato, peeled and diced (around 1½ cups)
- 2 cups shredded roasted chicken
- 1 cup fat free half-and-half or whole milk
- 4 cups uncooked wide egg noodles

Directions
- Over medium heat, melt the butter in a large pot or Dutch oven (4 quart or larger). Add the onion, carrots, celery, and garlic. Sauté for around 7 minutes or until the vegetables are soft. Add flour, oregano, pepper, thyme, and salt. Stir and cook for 3 minutes.
- Next, add the broth and potato. Give everything a quick stir, then increase the heat to medium-high. Bring the soup to a boil, without stirring, and boil for 3 minutes. Reduce the heat to medium-low, partially cover the pot, and allow to simmer for 25 minutes or until the potatoes have softened. Taste the soup. Add the chicken, milk/half-and-half, and noodles. Cook for 10 minutes until the noodles are tender and the soup has thickened. Once again, taste the soup and add more seasoning as desired.
- Serve the soup warm and enjoy!

Note: Cover and store leftovers in the refrigerator for up to 1 week. To reheat, simply pour into a pot over medium heat and cook until warm. Feel free to add more chicken broth to the leftovers if it's too thick.

Nutritional Information per serving Calories: 203.6 Fat: 4.1 g Carbohydrates: 20.1 g Protein: 20.3 g

Turkey Gumbo

Servings: 8 servings

Ingredients
- 4 cups unsalted turkey or chicken stock
- ⅛ tsp. ground allspice
- ⅛ tsp. ground cinnamon
- ⅛ tsp. ground coriander
- ⅛ tsp. smoked paprika
- ⅛ tsp. cayenne pepper
- ⅛ tsp. ground pepper
- ¼ cups canola oil
- ¼ cups all-purpose flour
- For serving: 2 cups of white rice
- Pinch of salt plus ¼ tsp., divided
- 2 stalks celery, finely chopped
- 1 medium sweet onion, finely chopped
- 1 medium red bell pepper, finely chopped
- 1 medium poblano pepper, finely chopped
- 3 cloves garlic, minced
- 1 (15 oz.) can no-salt-added diced tomatoes
- 2 cups shredded cooked turkey
- 8 oz. andouille sausage, chopped
- 4 oz. okra, thinly sliced
- 1 tbsp. chopped fresh thyme
- 2 bay leaves
- 1.5 tsp. filé powder
- ½ tsp. Worcestershire sauce

Directions
- Bring stock to a simmer in a large pot; keep warm. Combine allspice, cinnamon, coriander, paprika, cayenne and pepper in a small bowl.
- Meanwhile, heat oil in a large cast-iron skillet over medium-high heat. Whisk in flour and season with a pin. of salt. Cook, stirring often with a wooden spoon, until the roux is very brown, 2 to 4 minutes. Add celery, onion, bell pepper and poblano; cook, stirring occasionally, for 3 minutes. Add garlic; cook, stirring, for 1 minute. Add the spice mixture; cook, stirring, for 1 minute.
- Whisk the roux and vegetables into the hot broth until combined. Add tomatoes, turkey, sausage, okra, thyme, bay leaves, filé powder, Worcestershire, and the remaining 1/4 tsp. salt. Bring to a simmer.
- Reduce heat to maintain a simmer, cover and cook, stirring occasionally, for 30 minutes.

- Serve over rice and enjoy!

Nutritional Information per serving Calories: 232 Fat: 10.9 g Carbohydrates: 11.9 g Protein: 19.5 g

Chicken Sausage Gumbo

Servings: 10 servings

Ingredients
- 1 cup vegetable oil
- 1 cup all-purpose flour
- 1 large onion, chopped
- 1 large green bell pepper, chopped
- 2 celery stalks, chopped
- 1 lb. andouille or smoked sausage, sliced 1/4 in. thick
- 4 cloves garlic, minced
- Salt and pepper to taste
- Creole seasoning to taste
- 6 cups chicken broth
- 1 bay leaf
- 1 rotisserie chicken, boned and shredded
- For serving:
- 2 cups white rice

Directions
- Heat the oil in a Dutch oven over medium heat. When hot, whisk in flour. Continue whisking until the roux has cooked to the color of chocolate milk, 8 to 10 minutes. Be careful not to burn the roux. If you see black specks in the mixture, start over.
- Stir onion, bell pepper, celery, and sausage into the roux; cook for 5 minutes.
- Stir in the garlic and cook for another 5 minutes.
- Season with salt, pepper, and Creole seasoning; blend thoroughly.
- Pour in the chicken broth and add the bay leaf. Bring to a boil over high heat, then reduce heat to medium-low, and simmer, uncovered, for 1 hour, stirring occasionally.
- Stir in the chicken, and simmer for one hour more. Skim off any foam that floats to the top during the last hour.
- Serve over rice and enjoy!

Nutritional Information per serving Calories: 480 Fat: 39.5 g Carbohydrates: 14.1/2 g Protein: 16.1 g

Grilling

Turkey Burgers

Servings: 4 servings   **Serving size: 1 burger**

Ingredients
- 1 lb. ground turkey
- 1 large egg, beaten
- 2 cloves garlic, minced
- 1 tbsp. Worcestershire sauce
- 2 tbsps. freshly chopped parsley
- Kosher salt
- Freshly ground black pepper
- 1 tbsp. extra-virgin olive oil
- Hamburger buns
- Lettuce
- Sliced tomatoes
- Mayonnaise

Directions In a large bowl, mix together the ground turkey, egg, garlic, Worcestershire sauce, and parsley, then season with salt and pepper.
Once you have the ground mixture, form it into four flat patties.
Grab a medium skillet and heat over medium heat adding in some oil to grease the pan. Add patties over the heated oil and cook until the patties are golden giving them 5 minutes per side. Make sure the patties are cooked through.
Serve on a bun with desired toppings and enjoy!

Nutritional Information per serving Calories: 212 Fat: 14 g Carbohydrates: 0 g Protein: 22 g

Grilled Chicken Breast

Servings: 4 servings **Serving size: 1 chicken breast**

Ingredients
- 1¾ lb. boneless, skinless chicken breasts
- 6 tbsps. extra virgin olive oil
- 4 large garlic cloves, minced
- 1 tsp. dried thyme
- ½ tsp. dried oregano
- 1¼ tsp. salt
- ½ tsp. freshly ground black pepper
- 1½ tsps. lemon zest, from one lemon

Directions
- One at a time, place the chicken breasts in a 1-gallon Ziplock bag, using a meat mallet, pound to an even ½-in. thickness.
- Mix all the ingredients except for the chicken together in a 1-gallon Ziplock bag (go ahead and use the same one you used for pounding if it is still in good shape). Add the chicken breasts to the bag and massage the marinade into the meat until evenly coated. Seal the bag and place in a bowl in the refrigerator (the bowl protects against leakage); let the chicken marinate for at least 4 hours or overnight.
- Preheat the grill to high heat and oil the grates. Place the chicken breasts on the grill and cook, covered, for 2 to 3 minutes per side. Do not overcook.
- Transfer the chicken to a platter, serve, and enjoy!

Nutritional Information per serving Calories: 413 Fat: 25 g Carbohydrates: 2 g Protein: 42 g

Turkey Shish Kebabs

Servings: 4 kebabs **Serving size: 1 kebab**

Ingredients

For the marinade:
- 3 tbsps. olive oil
- ½ medium lemon, juice only
- 2 garlic cloves, minced
- ½ tsp. black pepper
- ½ tsp. cinnamon
- ½ tsp. paprika
- 1 tsp. salt
- 1 tsp. dried oregano

For the skewers:
- 17 oz. turkey chunks
- 1 red bell pepper, large
- 1 yellow bell pepper, large
- 1 onion, medium

Directions
- Place the marinade ingredients in a bowl that is large enough to hold all the meat. Give it a stir and add in the turkey chunks. Use your hands or a spoon to coat the meat with marinade. Cover with plastic wrap and refrigerate for 2-3 hours (or overnight).
- Cut the peppers and onion into chunks (similar size to the meat, if possible) and thread them as well as the turkey chunks onto the skewers (meat + pepper + onion + meat, etc.).
- Grill on medium to high heat for 10-15 minutes or until the meat is cooked through.
- Serve and enjoy!

Nutritional Information per serving Calories: 253 Fat: 12 g Carbohydrates: 8 g Protein: 27 g

Grilled Mojo Chicken

Servings: 4 servings **Serving size: 1 chicken breast**

Ingredients

For the chicken:
- 6-8 chicken thighs or 4 chicken breasts
- 1 red onion, peeled and thickly sliced
- 2 tbsps. olive oil

For the marinade:
- 1 orange, zested and juiced
- 2 limes, zested and juiced
- 3 cloves garlic, minced
- 2 tbsps. olive oil
- ½ cup white wine or chicken stock
- 1 tbsp. ground cumin
- 1 tsp. salt
- ¼ tsp. ground pepper

Directions Combine all marinade ingredients into a large Ziplock bag.
Reserve a quarter cup to baste the chicken as it grills.
Add chicken to the remaining marinade and let it rest for at least 20 minutes.
Rub olive oil on red onion slices and keep on a separate platter.
Heat the grill to high and place chicken and onions on the grill.
Reduce heat to medium-high. Cook for about 5-6 minutes on each side, basting with reserved marinade.
Chicken is done when internal temp reaches 165 degrees.

Nutritional Information per serving Calories: 427 Fat: 33 g Carbohydrates: 12 g Protein: 20 g

Chicken Sausage and Roasted Vegetables

Servings: 4 servings

Ingredients
- 1 lb. chicken sausage links, cut into ½-in. slices
- 1 medium zucchini, cut into 1-in. slices
- 1 medium yellow summer squash, cut into 1-in. slices
- 1 medium sweet red pepper, sliced
- 1 medium onion, cut into wedges
- 1 cup quartered fresh mushrooms
- ¼ cup olive oil
- 1 tbsp. dried oregano
- 1 tbsp. dried parsley flakes
- 1 tsp. garlic salt
- 1 tsp. paprika

Directions
- In a large bowl, combine the first six ingredients. In a small bowl, combine the oil, oregano, parsley, garlic salt, and paprika. Pour over sausage mixture; toss to coat. Divide between two pieces of heavy-duty foil (about 14 in. x 12 in.). Fold foil around the sausage mixture and seal tightly.
- Grill, covered, over medium heat for 25-30 minutes or until meat is no longer pink. Open foil carefully to allow steam to escape.
- Serve and enjoy!

Nutritional Information per serving Calories: 359 Fat: 29 g Carbohydrates: 12 g Protein: 14 g

Grilled Turkey Breast

Servings: 8 servings   **Serving size: 8 oz.**

Ingredients
- 3½-5 lbs. fresh turkey breast (may use a thawed frozen)
- For the brine (only if not injected or previously brined):
- water
- ¼ cup table salt
- ¼ cup brown sugar, optional
- 2-3 cloves crushed garlic, optional
- 2-3 bay leaves (optional)
- For the rub:
- 2 tablespoons brown sugar
- 1 tsp. kosher salt (only if not brining and not injected)
- 1 tsp. chili powder
- ½ tsp. oregano
- ½ tsp. cumin
- 2 tsps. oil

Directions

- If your turkey breast is not injected or previously brined, brining is an excellent idea. Start with a brine: 2 qt. of water and add ¼ cup each of salt and brown sugar. Crush 2-3 cloves of garlic and add 2-3 bay leaves (optional).
- Trim and clean a 3½ to 5-lb. turkey breast. Add the turkey to the brine and refrigerate for 3-6 hours.
- Preheat grill to a surface temperature of 350° to 400°. Mix a rub of 2 tablespoons brown sugar, 1 tsp. chili powder, ½ tsp. each oregano, and cumin. Add 1 tsp. kosher salt if you did not brine and if you are sure the breast was not injected.
- Rinse the breast carefully, pat dry then brush with a little oil. Apply the rub.
- Grill skin-side down for about 5-8 minutes to get some browning of the skin then flip and turn off the direct heat on that side of the grill with the meat. Place the thick side of the breast towards the heat. Keep the temp of the grill 350° to 375° in the area between the direct and indirect sides. Keep the lid closed and your hands off as much as possible.
- Cook until an internal temp of 165° in the thickest part and several other locations. This will vary by the weight and thickness of the turkey breast and your grill. Generally, about 1 ¾ to 2 hours). DO NOT COOK BY TIME ALONE.
- Remove from heat and let rest for 10 minutes before serving.

Nutritional Information per serving Calories: 266.4 Fat: 10.9 g Carbohydrates: 4.9 g Protein: 39.1 g

Pans and Ovens

Egg and Chicken Breakfast Bites

Servings: 6 servings   **Serving size:** 1 egg and chicken bite

Ingredients

- 1¼ cups liquid egg whites
- 1 large whole egg
- 2 Cajun chicken sausages, diced, (Brand: Nature's Promise only 2½ grams of fat per link)
- ¼ cup Jalapenos diced, and few slices 1 for topping each egg bite (1 pepper)
- ½ tsp. Black Pepper
- 1/2 tsp. Garlic Powder
- 1 dash Salt

Directions Preheat your oven to 350° F. Grease your muffin tin with a layer of cooking spray.
Add diced chicken sausage to a medium-sized bowl, diced jalapenos, black pepper, garlic powder, and salt. Stir until seasoning is evenly distributed among the sausage and vegetables.
Crack the whole egg and the liquid egg white into the bowl. Whisk together for 30 seconds to 1 minute.
Pour or scoop the sausage egg mixture into the greased muffin tins, filling them up to about ¾ of the way. Top each egg bite with one slice of jalapeno if desired
Bake in your preheated oven for 25 minutes. The egg muffins will puff up really high like a souffle and deflate when they are removed from the oven.

Note: You can allow them to cool completely, then portion out for breakfast.

Nutritional Information per serving Calories: 65 Fat: 1.7 g Carbohydrates: 1 g Protein: 10.6 g

Macro Chicken Pot Pie

Servings: 4 servings

Ingredients

- 1 tbsp. extra-virgin olive oil
- 10 oz. crimini baby bella mushrooms
- 1 cup diced carrots about 3 medium

- ½ cup diced celery about 1 large stalk
- 1½ tsps. garlic powder
- ½ tsp. kosher salt
- ¼ tsp. black pepper
- ¼ cup all-purpose flour
- 2 cups unsweetened almond milk
- 2 cups cooked and shredded boneless, skinless chicken breasts* about 8 oz. or 2 small breasts
- ½ cup frozen peas
- ½ cup frozen pearl onions
- 1 tbsp. chopped fresh thyme
- 1 prepared pie crust dairy-free if needed
- 1 egg lightly beaten with 1 tablespoon water to create an egg wash

Directions
- Preheat your oven to 425° F. Grease a 9-in. pie dish with baking spray and set aside to use later.
- Heat a large heavy-bottomed pan over medium-high heat; you may also use a Dutch oven or similar deep pan. Add the oil to the pan and heat. Add in the mushrooms and cook until they are beginning to brown, stirring occasionally, approx. 8 minutes. Add the rest of the vegetables and seasonings—carrots, celery, garlic powder, salt, and pepper.
- Cook until the mushrooms have browned, and the carrots begin to soften.
- Sprinkle in the flour and cook for 2 minutes. Gradually add the almond milk, a little at a time. Stir constantly. Bring to a low boil, scraping any brown bits from the bottom of the pan. Let mixture bubble until it thickens, about 3 to 5 minutes. Stir in the chicken, peas, onions, and thyme.
- Add the chicken mixture into the greased pie dish. Next, roll the pie dough into a circle large enough to cover your dish. Brush the edges of the pie dish with the egg wash, then lay the dough over the top so that it overhangs the sides. Trim the overhang to a ½ in. larger than the edge of the dish. Gently press the dough onto the sides of the dish so that it sticks, then brush it all over with the remaining egg wash. With a sharp knife, cut 3 slits in the top.
- Bake the pie until hot and bubbly on the inside and the crust is deeply golden brown, about 25 minutes. Let it rest for a few minutes.
- Serve hot and enjoy!

Nutritional Information per serving Calories: 380 Fat: 18 g Carbohydrates: 41 g Protein: 8 g

Oven-Roasted Turkey Legs

Servings: 8 servings   **Serving size: 1 leg**

Ingredients
- 4 large turkey legs
- 1 gallon water
- 1 cup + 1 tbsp. salt (divided)
- 2 sticks butter (softened)
- 1 tsp. black pepper
- 1 tsp. garlic powder
- 1 tsp. onion powder
- 1 tsp. dried thyme
- 1 tsp. paprika

Directions
- Whisk together the gallon of water with 1 cup of salt in a bucket and add the turkey legs. Let brine for 4 to 6 hours or overnight. (Note: It is best to stir the turkey legs halfway through the brining process). Remove from brine, rinse turkey legs under cool water, and pat dry with paper towels.
- Preheat the oven to 400° F and lay the turkey legs evenly on a sheet pan. Cut each stick of butter into 4 pieces (8 pieces total). Each turkey leg gets two pieces of butter. Slip one of the pieces of butter under the skin of each turkey leg. Rub the second piece of butter over the outside of the turkey leg. Repeat the process for the other 3 turkey legs.
- Combine the remaining tablespoon of salt with the rest of the spices and herbs and sprinkle liberally all over the turkey legs.
- Place in the oven and roast for 30 minutes. Rotate the pan, lower the oven to 300 degrees, and continue to roast for another 45 minutes to one hour until the outside is crispy and an internal temperature of 170 degrees is reached. Depending on the size of the turkey legs and the heat of the oven, more time may be required to cook the turkey legs all the way through.
- Remove from the oven and allow the turkey legs to rest for a few minutes before serving.

Nutritional Information per serving Calories: 961 Fat: 73 g Carbohydrates: 0 g Protein: 76 g

Macro Oven-Roasted Chicken

Servings: 6 servings   **Serving size: 1 piece of chicken**

Ingredients
- 1 2-3 lb. roasting chicken
- 1-2 tsps. kosher salt
- 1-2 tsps. ground black pepper
- 1-2 tsps. dried thyme

Directions
- Preheat your oven to 425° F.
- Remove the giblets from the inside of the chicken. They are not needed for this recipe so you can either save or discard them.
- Rinse the chicken, inside and out, and pat dry.
- Place chicken, breast-side down, on either an oven-safe fry pan or a rack in a roasting pan.
- Season the chicken liberally with salt, pepper, and dried thyme.
- If you want (and I totally recommend!), dice up some sweet potatoes and toss the cubes into the pan around the chicken while it roasts.
- Insert a meat thermometer set to 165 degrees into the deepest part of the thigh.
- Place the chicken in the oven and cook until the internal temperature reaches 165 degrees, approximately 45-60 minutes. (If you don't have a meat thermometer, you will know the chicken is done when the juices run clear between the leg and thigh when pierced with a fork.) Once done, carefully remove from the oven and allow to rest 5 minutes before slicing and serving.
- Serve and enjoy!

Nutritional Information per serving Calories: 486 Fat: 35.1 g Carbohydrates: 0. 9 g Protein: 38.9 g

General Tso's Macro Chicken

Servings: 4 servings

Ingredients
- 1½ lbs. boneless, skinless chicken breasts, cut into 1-in. chunks
- ¼ cup all-purpose flour
- 2 large eggs, beaten
- 2 cups crushed Corn Flakes

For the sauce:
- 1½ cups chicken broth
- ¼ cup hoisin sauce
- ¼ cup rice vinegar
- 3 tbsps. reduced sodium soy sauce
- 3 tbsps. brown sugar, packed
- 2 tbsps. cornstarch

Directions
- Preheat oven to 450° F. Coat a cooling rack with nonstick spray and place on a baking sheet; set aside.
- Working in batches, dredge chicken in flour, dip into eggs, then dredge in crushed Corn Flakes, pressing to coat.
- Place on a prepared baking sheet and coat with nonstick spray. Place in oven and bake until golden brown and crisp, about 13-15 minutes.
- In a large saucepan over medium high heat, combine chicken broth, hoisin, rice vinegar, soy sauce, brown sugar and cornstarch until thickened, about 1-2 minutes. Stir in chicken and gently toss to combine.
- Serve immediately and enjoy!

Nutritional Information per serving Calories: 275.2 Fat: 4.3 g Carbohydrates: 31.4 g Protein: 26.6 g

Chicken Katsu Don

Servings: 4 servings   **Serving size: 1 bowl**

Ingredients
- 1 piece of chicken Katsu
- 2 large eggs
- ¾ cup onion (~1/2 small onion)
- ⅓ cup dashi (or chicken stock)
- 2 tbsps. sake
- 1½ tbsps. soy sauce
- 2 tsps. evaporated cane sugar
- 1 serving cooked short-grain rice
- Mitsuba (or chopped scallions for garnish)

Directions
- If you are using leftover chicken katsu that's already been fried, move on to step 3. Otherwise, follow the instructions here for preparing and breading the chicken cutlets and come back to step 2 to fry it.
- Preheat 1½ in. of oil to 355° F. Fry the chicken, flipping it over at least once until the breading is golden brown (about 4-5 minutes). Transfer the katsu to a paper towel-lined rack and let it cool enough to handle.
- Cut the chicken katsu into ¾-in. slices. Break the eggs into a bowl and lightly beat them.
- Slice the onion thinly and add it to an 8-in. non-stick omelet pan, along with the dashi, sake, soy sauce, and sugar.
- Bring the onion mixture to a simmer and cook them until they are tender.
- Add the sliced cutlets and let them cook until they've soaked up the sauce on one side.
- Flip the chicken over and continue cooking until it's warmed through and fully cooked.
- Drizzle the beaten egg evenly over everything.
- Gently mix the egg with tongs or chopsticks, ensuring it flows between each piece of chicken and then slam the pan against the stove (don't do this if you have a glass-topped stove) to help redistribute the uncooked egg.
- Turn off the heat and allow the residual heat to cook the egg until it starts to turn opaque but is still creamy. If you want your eggs more thoroughly cooked, you can cover the pan with a lid before turning off the heat and let it steam.
- Serve and enjoy!

Nutritional Information per serving Calories: 679 Fat: 15 g Carbohydrates: 92 g Protein: 41 g

Chapter 6: Pork

Power in Pork

Pork is the most misunderstood of all the proteins due to its association with bacon and barbecue. This is unfair to pork because some cuts of pork have low saturated fat counts, and it is one of the best protein sources. Pork is a naturally sweet protein and pairs well with fruits and savory garnishes, making it one of the most delectable and satisfying proteins to pick for meals.

The main cuts that you will see in the recipes are pork tenderloin and pork shoulder, which is also called pork butt. These cuts of pork have the most protein with the least amount of saturated fats, making them perfect for the macro diet. Bacon comes from pork belly, which is the fattiest cut on the pig, and barbecue sauces tend to have large amounts of sugar, which is why barbecue is seen as unhealthy. There will be garnishes for some pork dishes. Still, these will be made from scratch or purchased considering the macro diet, as salad dressings were handled. The power in pork will be the power in you once you make these great pork dishes!

Shopping List

- Pork chops
- Pork loin
- Pork shoulder
- Pork necks
- Pork tenderloin
- Pork roast
- Pork butt
- Bacon
- Carrot
- Celery
- Celery stalk
- Tomatoes
- Avocado
- Baby spinach
- Yellow onion
- Red onion
- Parsnips
- Jalapenos
- Red potatoes
- Gold potatoes
- Prunes
- Pineapple
- Lemon
- Lime
- Olive oil
- Vegetable oil
- Fenugreek
- Honey
- White wine
- Red wine vinegar
- Balsamic vinegar
- Apple cider vinegar
- Honey
- Brown sugar
- Soy sauce
- Garlic paste
- Onion gravy
- Rice
- Flour tortillas
- All-purpose flour
- Salt
- Pepper
- Garlic
- Parsley
- Cumin
- Cardamon
- Cayenne pepper
- Jalapeno pepper powder
- Coriander
- Chicken base
- Thyme
- Rosemary
- Bay leaves
- Basil
- Oregano
- Hungarian paprika
- Smoked Paprika
- Onion powder
- Garlic powder
- Nutmeg
- Cilantro
- Red pepper flakes
- Chipotle chili powder
- Chili powder
- Dry mustard
- Green peppercorns
- Ginger
- Garlic pepper
- Cinnamon sticks
- Vegeta
- Butter
- Sour cream
- Worcestershire
- Tomato paste
- Can of diced tomatoes
- Canned chipotle peppers in adobo sauce
- Tomatillo

Stews

Pork Shoulder Green Chili Stew

Servings: 6 servings **Serving size: 1 bowl**

Ingredients
- Roasted Tomatillos and Peppers:
- 3 cups tomatillos cut in half,
- 2 cups Anaheim pepper, about 2 large peppers
- ⅓ cups Jalapenos, about 3 peppers
- ½ tbsps. extra virgin olive oil
- Pork Shoulder Preparation:
- 40. oz pork shoulder excess fat trimmed off, (about 2½ lbs.)
- 2 tbsps. all-purpose flour
- ½ tsp. salt
- ½ tbsp. black pepper
- 1 tbsp. extra virgin olive oil
- Putting it all Together into a Stew:
- 1 tsp. extra virgin olive oil
- ⅓ yellow onion, diced, about 1 onion
- 1½ tbsp. fresh garlic, about 5 cloves
- 24 oz. water
- ½ tsp. Cayenne pepper
- ¼ tsp. Jalapeno chili powder
- ½ tsp. ground coriander
- 2 tsps. reduced sodium chicken base
- 2 cups baby Yukon Gold potatoes cut in half (about 4 cups)
- Optional Toppings or Sides:
- Cherry tomatoes
- Avocado
- Red onion
- Lime
- Rice
- Flour tortillas

Directions

Roasted Tomatillos and Peppers:
- Preheat oven to 400° F. Line a baking sheet with tin foil and arrange your tomatillos and peppers on the tray. Drizzle with the oil, toss to coat, and bake for 20-25 minutes. Halfway through, turn everything over to allow browning on the other side.
- Once the peppers and tomatillos are blistered and charred, remove them from the oven and wrap them tightly in the foil to steam for 5-10 minutes to loosen up the skins for easy removal.
- After 10 minutes, open the foil, and remove and discard the skins and stems from the peppers and tomatillos. The pepper seeds contain most of the heat so remove them or leave some of them in if you like spicy. Chop the tomatillos and peppers and set aside.

Pork Shoulder Preparation:
- While the peppers and tomatillos are roasting, cut your pork shoulder into bite-sized cubes, removing any excess fat and heat a large heavy bottom pot or Dutch oven to medium heat.
- (If you leave too much fat on, a layer of fat will accumulate at the top of your stew. Don't remove it all, just the large sections.)
- Pat the pork cubes dry and place in a large bowl. Toss with pepper, salt, and flour, until the pork is evenly coated.
- Add the oil to the warmed pot. Working in batches (do not overcrowd the pot) cook the pork until browned on all sides, 3-4 minutes. Remove with a slotted spoon and transfer to a large bowl. Continue this until you have browned all the pork chunks.

Putting it all Together into a Stew:
- You have now browned your pork and pulled your tomatillos and peppers from the oven, steamed them, and peeled/removed the seeds.
- Now you will put it all together. Start with the large heavy bottom pot or Dutch oven that the pork was cooked in—do not clean, all that goodness at the bottom is going to add flavor to the stew.
- Turn the heat to medium, add the oil, onions, and garlic to the pot and cook until they are soft and translucent, 5-7 minutes.
- Add in the tomatillos and peppers and cook with the onions and garlic for 1 minute. Then add a few tablespoons of the water, using the water to deglaze the bottom of the pot, scraping the bottom of the pot with a heavy spatula.
- Now add the pork to the pot and season with the cayenne pepper, jalapeno pepper powder, and ground coriander. Stir everything together and cook for 3-5 minutes.
- Add the remainder of the water and the chicken base. Bring everything to a boil and cook for 5 minutes then turn the heat to low and allow to cook for 1–6 hours adding the potatoes 45 minutes before you plan to eat.

- (The longer the stew cooks, the more the flavors will develop. If planning to eat within one hour of adding the water and chicken base you can go ahead and add the potatoes right away. But if you have the time to allow the stew to simmer for hours then wait to add the potatoes until 45 minutes before eating.)
- Serve with any of your favorite toppings or sides and enjoy!

Nutritional Information per serving Calories: 543 Fat: 21.9 g Carbohydrates: 23.3 g Protein: 60 g

One Pot Pork Stew

Servings: 6 servings   **Serving size: 1 bowl**

Ingredients
- 2½ lbs. pork shoulder, trimmed of visible fat, cut into 1-in. cubes
- ½ cup all-purpose flour
- salt
- black pepper
- 2-4 tbsps. vegetable oil
- 4 slices bacon, chopped
- 1 large onion, diced
- 1 tbsp. garlic, minced
- 2 cups carrots, cut into ½ in. pieces
- 1 cup celery
- ½ cup white wine
- 4 cups beef broth
- 2 tbsps. tomato paste
- 1 tsp. dried thyme leaves
- ½ tsp. dried rosemary leaves
- 2 bay leaves
- ½ cup pitted prunes, chopped
- 2 russet potatoes, peeled and cubed
- 1 cup parsnips, peeled and diced
- Garnish (optional): 2-3 tablespoons parsley, chopped

Directions
- In a mixing bowl, toss the pork with the flour, 2 tsps. salt, and 1 tsp. black pepper to coat evenly, shaking off excess.
- Heat 2 tablespoons of oil, over medium-high heat, in a large pot and brown pork in batches without crowding it, about 7-9 minutes. Add more oil as needed. Transfer browned meat to a bowl with a slotted spoon and set aside. Remove and discard pan drippings.

Nutritional Information per serving Calories: 480 Fat: 20 g Carbohydrates: 43 g Protein: 30 g

Steamy Hungarian Pork Stew

Servings: 8 servings   **Serving size: 1 bowl**

Ingredients
- 8 medium yellow onions, chopped to medium dice
- ⅓ cup canola/vegetable oil, plus more for frying
- 9 ¾-in. thick boneless center cut loin pork chops, trimmed of fat
- 1 tbsp. salt
- 1 tbsp. pepper
- flour for dredging
- 3 tbsps. sweet Hungarian paprika
- 6-8 cups water, or enough to fully immerse all ingredients in the pot
- Vegeta to taste, approximately 1 tbsp. (or if you can't find it, use vegetable/chicken soup seasoning packets)
- 1 cup sour cream

Directions
- Add canola oil into a large pot (6 qt) over medium to medium-high heat. Add onions and sauté until they are translucent, but not browned. Add more oil when necessary to keep them slick in the process. Once onions are cooked, turn heat to low, add paprika to the mixture, and stir to mix well.
- Season the pork slices generously with salt and pepper then dredge them in flour on each side.
- Heat about one inch of canola or vegetable oil in a frying pan over medium-high to high heat. Fry each slice of pork until just barely golden brown around the edges, about 1-2 minutes, flipping halfway through. If they are thin enough, this will be enough to cook them fully. Lay them between sheets of paper towel on a plate to catch excess oil.
- Cut each of the pork slices in half and place them in the pot with the onions, adding enough water to cover. Cover pot and simmer on medium heat for 45 minutes to one hour. Stir occasionally.

- When the stew is thickened up a bit from the flour and the onions are starting to disappear, it is ready for the final seasoning. Add salt, pepper and Vegeta seasoning to taste. Add sour cream and stir until the stew is a rich, thick consistency.

Nutritional Information per serving Calories: 592 Fat: 36 g Carbohydrates: 17 g Protein: 49 g

Pulled Pork Stew

Servings: 4 servings   **Serving size: 8 oz.**

Ingredients
- 1½ lbs. pork neck bones
- ¼ tsp. salt
- ¼ tsp. black pepper, ground
- ¼ tsp. nutmeg, ground
- ¼ tsp. rosemary, dried
- ¼ tsp. onion powder
- 3 cloves garlic
- 3 tsps. olive oil
- 1 cup chicken broth
- 1½ tsps. apple cider vinegar
- ¼ tsp. bay leaf
- 2 tbsps. tomato paste
- 2 cups chicken broth, bouillon or consomme, homemade

Directions
- Place whole pork neck bones in the base of a cast iron double boiler or a simple large soup pot. Sprinkle the salt, pepper, nutmeg, rosemary, and onion powder over the neck bones. Crush the garlic cloves and add them to the pot before drizzling olive oil over all the ingredients. Turn the heat on your stove to medium heat and stir the neck bones around to get them all coated in the oil and spices. Use a pair of tongs to occasionally rotate the neck bones while they sear to a golden brown. Put a lid over your pot between rotations to help the fat collect.
- Once your neck bones are golden brown, pour in the first amount of chicken broth and apple cider vinegar. Place 2 whole bay leaves in the broth before closing the pot with a lid. Turn the heat to a low setting and let the pork cook for up to one hour—until the meat easily slides off the bones. Cook longer if necessary.
- Use your tongs to pull the meat off the bones and break it up into shreds and small chunks. You may also remove the pork from the pot, pull it off the bones, and return the meat to the pot. Either discard the neck bones or save them for making your own soup broth/stock! You may also discard any large pieces of fat that are unappetizing to you.
- With the stove heat still on low, stir in the tomato paste and final amount of chicken broth. Put the lid on and raise the heat to bring the stew to a boil.
- Once at a boil, reduce to a strong simmer and leave the lid off the pot. Cook openly while stirring occasionally until the liquid reduces to a thick stew—about 15-20 minutes. Remove the bay leaves before serving!

Nutritional Information per serving Calories: 595 Fat: 30.6 g Carbohydrates: 3.8 g Protein: 71.4 g

Root Vegetable and Pork Stew

Servings: 6 servings   **Serving size: 1 bowl**

Ingredients
- 2½ lbs. boneless pork roast, cut into one inch cubes
- ¼ cup all-purpose flour
- 1½ tsps. salt, divided
- 1½ tsps. black pepper, divided
- 1 tsp. smoked paprika
- 3 tbsps. olive oil
- 1 large yellow onion, chopped
- 4 garlic cloves, minced
- 1 cup white wine (or chicken broth)
- 2 celery stalks, cut into ½-in. chunks
- 5 carrots, peeled and cut into ½-in. chunks
- 4 medium Yukon gold potatoes, peeled and cut into 1" chunks
- 2 cups chicken broth
- 14.5 oz. can of diced tomatoes
- 2 tbsps. Worcestershire sauce
- 2 bay leaves
- 1 tsp. dried basil
- ½ tsp. dried oregano
- 8 oz. Baby Bella mushrooms, chopped
- 1 cup frozen peas
- 1 bunch parsley, chopped for garnish

Directions
- Whisk together flour, ½ tsp. salt, ½ tsp. black pepper, and paprika in a medium bowl then toss the pork cubes in it until coated, coating pork in seasoned flour.
- Heat olive oil over medium heat in a large Dutch oven.
- Once oil is hot, place the pork in an even layer on the bottom of the pan. You may need to do this process in 2-3 batches depending upon the size of your Dutch oven and amount of pork used, frying pork cubes in Dutch oven.
- Brown the pork for 2-3 minutes on each side until all pieces are browned and then transfer to a plate.
- Add the onion to the pan and sauté for 1 minute then add the garlic and cook for another 30 seconds stirring as it cooks.
- Add the wine or equal amounts of broth to the Dutch oven and stir while scraping the bottom of the pan to deglaze any cooked bits from the pot.
- Add the celery, carrots, potatoes, chicken broth, tomatoes, and Worcestershire sauce and stir to combine, adding potatoes and tomatoes to Dutch oven.
- Add the bay leaves, dried basil, dried oregano, remaining salt and black pepper, then stir.
- Bring the mixture to a boil, then reduce the heat and simmer for 45 minutes.
- Add the pork back to the Dutch oven, stir and cover simmering for 30-40 minutes stirring occasionally.
- Add the mushrooms and frozen peas to the stew and simmer uncovered for an additional 10-15 minutes or until the mushrooms are tender, adding mushrooms and peas to pork stew.
- Season with additional salt and pepper if needed, then serve with a slice of bread and fresh parsley on top.

Nutritional Information per serving Calories: 854 Fat: 48 g Carbohydrates: 46 g Protein: 52 g

Pepper Pork Stew

Servings: 6 servings **Serving size: 1 bowl**

Ingredients
- 2 lbs. pork butt, diced
- 1 small onion, diced
- 3 cloves garlic, crushed
- 2 tbsps. green peppercorns
- 2 tsps. ground ginger
- 2 tsps. cracked black pepper
- 2 tsps. cumin, ground
- 1 tsp. fenugreek, ground
- ½ tsp. cardamom, ground
- 1 cinnamon stick
- 8 oz. tomato passata
- ½ cup sour cream
- ⅓ cup heavy cream
- 4 oz. baby spinach
- ⅓ cup cilantro, torn

Directions Combine all the ingredients, except the sour cream, heavy cream, spinach, and cilantro, in your slow cooker.
Mix well. Cook on low for 8 hours or high for 4 hours, until the pork is tender.
Discard the cinnamon stick and add the heavy cream, spinach, and half the cilantro.
Cook on high for 5-10 minutes, until the spinach wilts.
Serve immediately with a side of cauliflower rice, sprinkled with the remaining cilantro.

Nutritional Information per serving Calories: 315 Fat: 8 g Carbohydrates: 7 g Protein: 27 g

Grilling

Pork Tenderloin and Chimichurri Sauce

Servings: 6-8 servings   **Serving size: 100 g of pork tenderloin with 30 g of chimichurri**

Ingredients

For the Pork:
- 2½ lbs. pork tenderloin
- 6 cloves of garlic
- 2 tbsps. brown sugar
- 1 tbsp. balsamic vinegar
- 1 tbsp. olive oil
- 1 tsp. chili powder
- 1 tsp. cumin
- 1 tsp. kosher salt

For the Chimichurri:
- 1 cup fresh cilantro
- ¾ cup fresh basil leaves
- ¼ cup white balsamic vinegar
- 2 tbsps. fresh lemon juice
- 2 cloves of garlic
- ½ tbsp. olive oil
- ½ tsp. salt
- ¼ tsp. pepper
- A pinch of red pepper flakes

Directions Prepare the vegetables as listed above.
Preheat the grill to high heat.
Trim the fat off the tenderloins.
Mix all the other ingredients for the pork in a bowl. Using gloves, rub the pork thoroughly with the marinade.
Spray grill with cooking spray, being careful not to burn yourself with the flames.
Place the tenderloins on the grill and cook for about 2-3 minutes per side. Lower heat to medium and cover. Cook for about 15-17 minutes, rotating every five minutes. Internal temperature should reach 140° F.
Place all the chimichurri ingredients in a blender and pulse until fully incorporated.
Allow the tenderloins to rest for 10 minutes while over a tent of aluminum foil.
Cut the tenderloins to proportion sizes and drizzle with chimichurri.
Serve and enjoy!

Nutritional Information per serving Calories: 207 Fat: 6.2 g Carbohydrates: 8.7 g Protein: 28.2 g

Grilled Pork with Soy Sauce Marinade

Servings: 4 servings   **Serving size: 1 pork chop**

Ingredients

- 4 thick bone-in or boneless pork chops (1 in. thick)
- For the marinade:
- ¼ cup soy sauce (see notes)
- ¼ cup fresh lime juice (see notes)
- ¼ cup olive oil
- 1 tsp. ground cumin (or a little less if you're not a big cumin fan)
- ½ tsp. dried oregano (see notes)
- A pinch of Chipotle chili powder (or use a dash of hot sauce)
- ½ tsp. onion powder (or use 1-2 tsp. grated fresh onion)
- ½ tsp. garlic powder (or use 1-2 tsp. freshly minced garlic)

Directions
- Trim visible fat from pork chops as much as desired. For thick boneless pork chops I would pound with a meat mallet, (or anything heavy) until pork chops are about ¾ in. thick. Bone-in pork chops won't need that.
- Combine soy sauce (gluten-free if needed), fresh lime juice, olive oil, ground cumin, dried oregano, Chipotle chili powder, onion powder, and garlic powder to make the marinade.
- Put pork chops in a heavy Ziplock bag or plastic dish with a lid, then pour marinade over. Let pork chops marinate 4-6 hours in the refrigerator. (They can be marinated all day while you're at work too.)
- When you're ready to cook, take pork chops out of the refrigerator, drain off the marinade, and let them come to room temperature while you preheat the grill.

- For an outdoor gas or charcoal grill, spray grill grates with non-stick spray or olive oil; then preheat the grill to medium-high before you start to cook. (You can only hold your hand there for a few seconds at that heat.)
- If you're using a stove-top grill pan (affiliate link) or a George Foreman Grill (affiliate link), heat just for a few minutes then brush or spray with non-stick spray or olive oil.
- To get criss cross grill marks, lay the pork chops at an angle across the grill grates for 3-4 minutes, then lift up the edge to check the grill marks and rotate pork chops the opposite way and cook 3-4 minutes more.
- When you have good criss cross marks, turn pork chops over and cook for about 3-5 minutes on the other side. Start to check pork after about 3 minutes. I highly recommend using an Instant-Read Meat Thermometer (affiliate link) to check that pork has reached the safe temperature of 145°F/63°C that's recommended for grilled pork but if you don't have a meat thermometer, pork should feel firm but not hard to the touch when it's done.
- Remember that the George Foreman grill cooks both sides at once, so grilling time is about half as long for that kind of grilling device. Grilled meats continue to cook for a few minutes when you take them off the grill, so don't overcook.
- Serve hot and enjoy!

Nutritional Information per serving Calories: 215 Fat: 18 g Carbohydrates: 3 g Protein: 11 g

Grilled Pork Tenderloin

Servings: 6 servings

Serving size: 1 tenderloin

Ingredients
- 2 whole pork tenderloin 1lb each
- For the Marinade
- ¼ cup olive oil
- ⅓ cup coconut aminos
- ¼ cup red wine vinegar
- 1 tbsp. Worcestershire sauce
- ½ juice of a lemon
- 1 tsp. dry mustard
- 1 tbsp. fresh cracked black pepper
- ½ tsp. salt
- 6 cloves garlic minced
- 1 tbsp. rosemary

Directions

For the marinade:
- Combine all ingredients and whisk together until combined well.
- Place tenderloins into a container or Ziplock bag and pour marinade into the bag.
- Move around until marinade has coated tenderloins and refrigerate for up to 8 hours, but at least 2 hours before grilling.

Grilling the Pork Tenderloins:
- Remove the tenderloins from the refrigerator one hour before grilling.
- Heat your grill to a medium high heat.
- Once to temperature, add tenderloins to grill.
- Grill tenderloins, turning every 1-2 minutes until the pork has preferred char and has reached an internal temperature of 140°F. Remove from direct heat and allow it to finish with indirect heat if needed.
- Remove from the grill, tent with aluminum foil, and rest for 10 minutes.

Nutritional Information per serving Calories: 207 Fat: 6.2 g Carbohydrates: 8.7 g Protein: 28.2 g

Spiced Pork Chops

Servings: 4 servings

Serving size: 1 pork chop

Ingredients
- 2 tbsps. olive oil
- 1 tbsp. Worcestershire sauce
- 1 tsp. lemon juice
- 1 tsp. paprika
- ½ tsp. onion powder
- ½ tsp. ground cumin
- ½ tsp. garlic paste
- Salt and pepper
- 4 boneless pork chops

Directions
- In a large plastic bag add everything except for the pork. Squish it around to mix everything together.
- Add the boneless pork chops and massage the marinade sauce around the meat.
- Season the chops with salt and pepper on both sides and discard the sauce. Cook the chops on a preheated grill pan until cooked through, about 4-5 minutes on each side.
- Serve with salad, horseradish coleslaw, or both!

Nutritional Information per serving Calories: 277 Fat: 16 g Carbohydrates: 1 g Protein: 29 g

Rosemary Lime Butter Pork Chops

Servings: 4 servings **Serving size: 1 pork chop**

Ingredients
- Four 1-in. cut bone-in pork chops
- Salt and pepper for seasoning
- ¼ cup butter (can be melted or softened)
- 1 tbsp. chopped fresh rosemary
- 1 tbsp. lime juice
- 1 tsp. garlic paste or 1 clove of minced garlic
- ½ tsp. fresh thyme
- A pinch of red pepper flakes

Directions
- Preheat the grill. If you have a gas grill, turn it to high heat. If you have a charcoal grill, set the grill for partial direct high heat. Once the grill is hot, clean the grates by wiping them with cooking oil. Heat grill thermometer to a high heat setting
- Generously season all sides of the pork chops with salt and pepper at least 30 minutes prior to cooking.
- Prepare the rosemary lime butter. Add all remaining ingredients to a small bowl. Mix to combine.
- Place the pork chops on the hot side of the grill about 3 inches apart and grill over direct heat for about 2 minutes each side.
- When chops are seared on all sides, move them to indirect heat (the colder side of the grill), top with half of the rosemary lime butter and let cook for 5-6 minutes or until the internal temperature of the chops reaches 145°F. Add a dollop of combined butter mixture on top of each pork chop
- Remove from the grill. Flip pork chops over, top with remaining butter and let rest for 10 minutes before serving.

Nutritional Information per serving Calories: 319 Fat: 23 g Carbohydrates: 0.3 g Protein: 23.1 g

Pork Chops Al Pastor

Servings: 4 servings **Serving size: 1 pork chop**

Ingredients

For the pork chops:
- 4 pork chops (about 6 oz. each)
- 2 tbsps. canned chipotle peppers in adobo sauce
- 1 tsp. ground cumin
- ⅛ tsp. ground cloves
- ½ tsp. kosher salt
- 1 tsp. dried oregano leaves
- 1 tbsp. apple cider vinegar
- 1 tbsp. olive oil

For the butter:
- ½ cup salted butter (1 stick), softened
- ¼ cup chopped fresh pineapple
- 2 tbsps. minced red onion
- 1 tsp. minced fresh garlic
- 1 tbsp. minced fresh cilantro
- 1 tbsp. lime zest
- 1 tbsp. granulated erythritol sweetener (optional)

Directions

For the pork chops:
- Combine the chipotle peppers, cumin, cloves, oregano, salt, vinegar and oil in a small blender cup and blend until smooth.
- Coat the pork chops in the marinade.
- Cover and marinate in the refrigerator for at least 2 hours, or overnight.
- Remove the pork chops from the refrigerator 30 minutes before ready to grill.
- Prepare and preheat the grill to about 400°F.
- Grill the pork chops over direct heat for about 3 minutes per side, or until a thermometer inserted in the thickest part reads 145°F.
- Remove to a clean platter and top each pork chop with 2 tablespoons of the butter mixture.
- Serve warm.

For the butter:
- Combine all the butter ingredients in a medium bowl and blend with a fork or spatula until fully mixed.
- Store leftover butter in an airtight container in the refrigerator for up to 5 days, or in the freezer for up to 3 months.
- If frozen, thaw for 30 minutes before using.

Nutritional Information per serving Calories: 495 Fat: 47 g Carbohydrates: 1 g Protein: 25 g

Pans and Ovens

Garlic Butter Baked Pork

Servings: 4 servings **Serving size: 1 pork chop**

Ingredients
- 2 medium-sized pork chops (I like to recommend pork chops from ButcherBox because it's heritage breed pork)
- Salt and pepper
- 4 tbsps. melted butter—you can also use ghee.
- 1 tbsp. fresh thyme, chopped
- 2 cloves garlic, minced
- 1 tbsp. extra virgin olive oil

Directions
- Preheat the oven to 375°F. Season the pork chops with salt and pepper and set aside.
- In a small bowl, mix together the butter, thyme, and garlic. Set aside.
- In a cast iron skillet, heat the olive oil over medium heat. When the skillet is really hot, add the pork chops. Sear until golden, about 2 minutes per side.
- Pour the garlic butter mixture over the pork chops. Place the skillet in the oven, and cook until the pork chops reach an internal temperature of 145°F, about 10-14 minutes. The time depends on the thickness of your pork chops.
- Remove from the oven. Using a spoon, pour some of the butter sauce left in the skillet onto the pork chops before serving.

Nutritional Information per serving Calories: 371 Fat: 35 g Carbohydrates: 1 g Protein: 14 g

Baked Pork Chops with Gravy and Potatoes

Servings: 4 servings **Serving size: 1 pork chop**

Ingredients

- 6 medium red-skinned potatoes, thinly sliced
- 1 medium onion, chopped
- 1 (12 oz.) jar zesty onion gravy
- 4 (3 oz.) boneless pork loin chops, trimmed of fat
- ½ tsp. garlic-pepper blend

Directions
- Heat oven to 350°F. Spray 13x9-in. (3-quart) baking dish with nonstick cooking spray. Arrange potato slices in sprayed baking dish; top with onion. Pour gravy over potatoes and onion. Cover tightly with foil.
- Bake for 30 to 35 minutes or until potatoes are tender.
- Meanwhile, sprinkle both sides of pork chops with garlic-pepper blend. Spray a large nonstick skillet with nonstick cooking spray. Heat over medium-high heat until hot. Place chops in pan. Cook 1 to 2 minutes on each side or until browned.
- Place pork chops over potato mixture. Cover; bake an additional 15 to 20 minutes or until pork is no longer pink.

Nutritional Information per serving Calories: 390 Fat: 8 g Carbohydrates: 53 g Protein: 27 g

Juicy Skillet Pork Chops

Servings: 4 servings **Serving size: 1 pork chop**

Ingredients
- 4 pork chops, about 1-in. thick and 6 to 7 oz. each, see notes
- Salt, to taste
- 1 tbsp. all-purpose flour
- 1 tsp. chili powder, see our homemade chili powder recipe
- 1 tsp. garlic powder
- 1 tsp. onion powder
- ½ tsp. smoked paprika
- ½ tsp. ground black pepper
- 1 tbsp. olive oil
- 1 cup low-sodium chicken stock, see our homemade chicken stock recipe
- 1 tbsp. apple cider vinegar
- 2 tsps. honey or brown sugar
- 1 tbsp. butter
- 2 tbsps. chopped fresh parsley, optional

Directions

For the pork chops:
- Take the pork chops out of the refrigerator and season on both sides with salt and pepper—we use just less than ¼ tsp. of fine salt per pork chop. Set the chops aside to rest for 30 minutes.
- To prepare the spice rub, mix the flour, chili powder, garlic powder, onion powder, and smoked paprika in a small bowl. After 30 minutes, use a paper towel to pat the pork chops dry then rub both sides of the chops with the spice rub.
- Heat the oil in a medium skillet (with lid) over medium-high heat. As soon as the oil is hot and looks shimmery, add the pork. Cook until golden, 2 to 3 minutes.
- Turn the pork seared side facing up. (If there is a fattier side of the pork, use kitchen tongs to hold the chops, fat-side-down until it sizzles and browns slightly; about 30 seconds.) Reduce heat to low and place a lid on the skillet. Cook 6 to 12 minutes or until an instant-read thermometer reads 145° F when inserted into the thickest part of the chop. (Since cooking time depends on the thickness of the chops, check for doneness at 5 minutes then go from there, checking every 2 minutes). If you do not have a thermometer, you will know they are done if when cutting into the chops, the juices run clear.
- Transfer pork chops to a plate then cover loosely with aluminum foil. Let the pork rest for 5 minutes.

For the pan sauce:
- While the pork rests, make the pan sauce. Increase the heat to medium-high then add the chicken stock, vinegar, and honey. Use a wooden spoon to scrape the bottom of the pan so that any stuck bits of pork come up. Simmer until reduced by half. Taste, then adjust the seasoning with salt, more vinegar, or honey. Move the skillet off the heat and when the sauce stops simmering, add the butter. Place the pork chops back into the pan and spoon some of the sauce on top. Or you may slice the chops then put them back into the pan.

Nutritional Information per serving Calories: 369 Fat: 14.3 g Carbohydrates: 11.6 g Protein: 46.1 g

Pan Roasted Pork Loin

Servings: 6 servings   **Serving size: 1/6 of the dish**

Ingredients
- 3 lbs. pork loin roast (NOT tenderloin)
- ¼ cup olive oil
- ¼ cup low sodium soy sauce
- ¼ cup Worcestershire sauce
- ¼ cup apple cider vinegar
- 2 tsps. dry ground mustard
- 1 tbsp. garlic powder
- 2 tbsps. fresh chopped parsley

Directions
- Preheat oven to 425°F.
- In a large mixing bowl whisk together all ingredients, except pork, to combine.
- Rinse and pat roast dry. Place in the marinade mixture, turning to coat all sides and rubbing the mixture into the meat.
- Heat a cast iron (or other heavy bottomed, oven safe skillet) over medium-high heat. Place the meat in the hot skillet. Using two sets of tongs, turn the meat every two minutes until all sides have a nice sear, and leave it fat side up. Slide into the preheated oven. Do not pierce with a fork to flip.
- Roast pork for about 30 minutes, or until a thermometer inserted into the center of the pork reads 145°F.
- Remove from the oven and transfer pork to a cutting board. Tent with foil and let rest for 10-15 minutes before slicing and serving.

Nutritional Information per serving Calories: 404 Fat: 18 g Carbohydrates: 4 g Protein: 52 g

Classic Baked Pork Chops

Servings: 4 servings   **Serving size: 1 pork chop**

Ingredients
- 4 bone-in pork chops, trimmed of fat
- 2 tbsps. extra-virgin olive oil
- Kosher salt
- Freshly ground black pepper
- 4 sprigs fresh rosemary
- Roasted potatoes, for serving

Directions
1. Preheat oven to 400° F. Rub pork chops with olive oil and season generously with salt and pepper. Set a cast-iron skillet over medium-high heat on the stovetop to heat up, 5 minutes.
2. Add pork chops to skillet and sear 3 minutes, then flip. Add rosemary sprigs to skillet then transfer to oven and continue cooking until no longer pink, 6 to 8 minutes.
3. Serve with roasted potatoes and enjoy!

Nutritional Information per serving Calories: 160 Fat: 6 g Carbohydrates: 0 g Protein: 23 g

Chapter 7: Beef

The King of Meat

Who doesn't love a good steak or beef stew? Beef is considered by many to be the prime of all meats, and with the number of burgers, steaks, hot dogs, and beef recipes for simple foods that are readily available, it's not hard to see why. Beef is the king of meat due to its simple preparation, robust flavor, and is a luxury item in many countries. Like other animal products, beef is high in protein. It has excellent benefits for those looking to fill the stomach and please the spirit.

That said, beef's reputation also comes with its flaws. Beef is the most accessible animal product with the highest amounts of saturated fats. It is a significant contributor to bad cholesterol. The entire book focuses on balancing what you do and what you eat. Beef should be treated like the animal protein you consume the least due to these detrimental effects. Pork's association with processed foods, bacon, and fast food is what gave it its reputation. In contrast, despite being worse, beef seems to have its health detriments swept under the rug.

That's not to say that beef should be avoided unless you choose to do so. It's just best to view beef as the one animal protein you consume the least when doing the Macro diet. As with pork, the cut of meat is also essential. Cuts with more protein will be prioritized over cuts with less protein and higher fat content. Remember, beef is the king of meat, and it's best not to overindulge like a king for the sake of your health. That said, here are some of the best Macro diet beef recipes for your enjoyment.

A Note on Grilling Steaks

As with poultry, eating raw or undercooked beef can cause foodborne illnesses to spread through your body. Grilled steaks can be safe to eat if cooked to the right temperature. Still, it's best to avoid or sparingly eat rare and medium-rare cooked steaks, as these are more likely to contain microbes that carry foodborne illnesses. The best way to prevent this (aside from not eating steaks) is to check the freshness and quality of the beef you consume before preparation. If it's not up to standard, it's best to throw it away. Steak enthusiasts may be disappointed to read this, but it's best to do what's suitable for your health before you do what's right for your palette.

Shopping List

- Beef round
- Onions
- Curry paste
- Red potatoes
- Carrots
- White rice
- Sirloin steaks
- Red bell pepper
- Yellow bell pepper
- Green bell pepper
- Small mushrooms
- Red onion slices
- Red wine vinegar
- Olive oil
- Oregano
- Garlic powder
- Onion powder
- Black pepper
- Worcestershire sauce
- Salt
- Avocado oil
- Coconut aminos
- Dijon mustard
- Rosemary
- Lemon
- Black pepper
- Flank steak
- Chuck roast
- Sweet potatoes
- Dale's low sodium seasoning
- Butter
- Beef bouillon cubes
- Dry onion soup mix
- Balsamic vinegar

Stews

Japanese Steak Curry

Servings: 6 servings   **Serving size: 1 bowl**

Ingredients
- 1½ lbs beef round
- 1 large raw onion
- 4 tsp. curry paste
- 3 chopped red potatoes
- 3 large chopped carrots
- 3 cups of water
- 3 cups long-grain white rice

Directions
- Cook rice according to package directions.
- Meanwhile, dice beef into 1 inch pieces.
- Dice one large onion.
- In a large skillet, sauté meat and onion in oil until lightly browned, about 3 minutes. Add carrots and potatoes. Discard excess oil.
- Add 3 cups of water and bring to a boil. Reduce heat, cover and simmer until meat and potatoes are tender, about 10 minutes.
- Add curry and sauté to coat.
- Simmer for about 5 minutes, stirring constantly (if curry sauce becomes too thick, just add water).

Nutritional Information per serving Calories: 628 Fat: 10.2 g Carbohydrates: 97.1/2 g Protein: 33.8 g

Grilling

Beef Shish Kebabs

Servings: 8 kebabs   **Serving size: 1 kebab**

Ingredients
- 1½ lbs. sirloin steaks
- 3 oz. red bell pepper
- 3 oz. yellow bell pepper
- 3 oz. green bell pepper
- 8 small mushrooms
- 4 oz. red onion slices
- For the marinade:
- 3 tbsps. red wine vinegar
- 2 tbsps. olive oil
- 1 tbsp. oregano
- 1 tsp. garlic powder
- 1 tsp. onion powder
- 1 tsp. black pepper
- 1 tsp. Worcestershire sauce
- ½ tsp. salt

Directions
- Mix the marinade ingredients into a Ziplock bag then add the chopped steak pieces.
- Marinate the beef in the fridge for at least 4-12 hours for best results; a shorter time will result in less flavor.
- After the minimum 4 hours marinate time is up, thread the beef and vegetables onto the kabob skewers; do not pack them too tightly.
- Preheat a grill to medium-high heat.
- Brush the grill grates with oil. Grill the kabobs directly over the heat, turning occasionally and basting with remaining marinade for 5 to 10 minutes, or until cooked to your preference.
- Serve and enjoy!

Nutrition Information per serving Calories: 168 Fat: 7 g Carbohydrates: 4 g Protein: 19 g

Classic Steak Dinner

Servings: 8 servings   **Serving size: ⅛ of the steak**

Ingredients
- ¾ cup avocado oil
- ½ cup coconut aminos
- 2 tbsps. Dijon mustard
- 2 tbsps. fresh chopped rosemary
- 1 lemon zest and juice
- 1 tbsp. minced garlic
- 1½ tsps. salt
- ½ tsp. fresh ground black pepper
- 2 lbs. flank steak

Directions
- Combine the avocado oil, coconut aminos, Dijon mustard, rosemary, lemon juice and zest, garlic, salt, and pepper in a blender. Process until smooth.
- Place the steak in a zip-top bag and pour the marinade over.
- Marinate for at least 1 hour and up to 4 hours. (If you want to marinate overnight, omit the lemon.)
- Preheat the grill to medium-high. Add the flank steaks and grill for about 3 to 5 minutes per side, until an instant-read thermometer inserted in the thickest part registers 120° F for medium-rare and 130° F for medium.
- Transfer to a cutting board. Allow to rest for 5 minutes and then slice against the grain.
- Serve and enjoy!

Nutrition Information per serving Calories: 360 Fat: 26.3 g Carbohydrates: 5 g Protein: 24.7 g

Pans and Ovens

Macro Roast Beef

Servings: 8 servings   **Serving size: ⅛ of a serving**

Ingredients
- 3 lbs. chuck roast
- 1 ½ carrots (either baby or peeled and cut into 3 in. pieces) (approx. 1 small bag or half of a large bag)
- 4 sweet potatoes, washed and quartered
- 1 large onion, quartered
- 1 tbsp. Dale's low sodium seasoning
- 1 tbsp. butter
- 4 beef bouillon cubes
- 2 tbsps. dry onion soup mix
- 1 tbsp. Worcestershire sauce
- 1 tbsp. balsamic vinegar
- 1 tbsp. minced garlic
- 1 can Cream of Whatever soup (optional)

Directions
- Add veggies to the bottom of the pot. Then place meat on top. Mix seasonings and sauces in a bowl (smush up the bouillon cubes) and pour over meat. Cook on high for 3-4 hours or on low for 6-8 hours. It's done when the meat falls apart with a fork.
- You can add a can of cream of whatever soup to the seasonings and sauces if you'd like to have gravy with it. (I make my own).
- Trim roast and discard as much fat as you can. Divide into 8 servings immediately. I always ladle some of the au jus it creates into the storage containers to keep it from drying out.

Nutrition Information per serving Calories: 423 Fat: 13 g Carbohydrates: 26 g Protein: 48 g

Chapter 8: Seafood

Gifts from the Sea

Seafood is the best animal protein source. Unlike the other animal protein sources, the fats from seafood products are all unsaturated. As stated before, unsaturated fats can lower bad cholesterol by raising good cholesterol. Not bad! It's also not surprising to see that the country that eats the most seafood, Japan, also has one of the world's highest life expectancy rates. That's also where the modern Macro diet was born. You should take advantage of seafood and make it the one protein you consume more often than others, barring dietary restrictions.

That said, seafood does come with some detriments, and it is important to name them before going forward. First, like poultry, seafood must be handled and prepared with care because some of the worst foodborne illnesses can come from seafood. Salmonella was so named due to where it was first found. There's also mercury in many seafood products. Mercury isn't harmful to most people if consumed in small quantities. Still, the most significant concerns are for pregnant women, women planning to be pregnant, and children below six. Mercury can damage kidneys and the nervous system, cause learning disabilities for children, and lead to pregnancy complications or deformities. The best way to avoid that is by knowing which fish has the highest mercury levels and avoid eating them altogether. The simplest way to know which fish to avoid is to see how high up the food chain is. The higher you go, the more mercury there is. One of the most common fish for consumption, tuna, falls under this category as well, so it's best to limit your consumption of these fish for your own health. That said, the gifts from the sea are waiting for you in these beautiful recipes.

Shopping List

- Dry sea scallops
- Salmon
- Shrimp
- Tomatoes
- Bell pepper
- Cucumber
- Red onion
- Fresh cilantro
- Garlic
- Chopped parsley
- Chopped basil
- Italian seasoning
- Red wine vinegar
- Salt
- Ground pepper
- Whole wheat bread
- Extra-virgin olive oil
- Butter
- Lime
- Lemon
- Whole grain or wild rice with quinoa

Grilling

Gazpacho with Scallop Skewers (Carbohydrates)

Servings: 4 servings   **Serving size:** 11/4 cups of Gazpacho, 4 oz. of scallops.

Ingredients
- 1¼ lbs. dry sea scallops
- 5 cups tomatoes
- 1½ cups chopped bell pepper
- 1½ cups cucumber
- ½ cup red onion
- ¼ cup fresh cilantro
- 2 cloves garlic
- 2 tbsps. red-wine vinegar
- ¼ tsp. salt
- ½ tsp. ground pepper and ⅛ tsp., divided for separate uses
- 1 cup whole-wheat bread
- 2 tbsps. extra-virgin olive oil
- 2 tbsps. unsalted butter
- ½ tsp. lime zest

Directions
- Chop red onion, bell peppers, cilantro, cucumber, garlic, and tomatoes.
- Combine diced vegetables with vinegar, salt, and ½ tsp of black pepper in a blender or food processor.
- Pulse until chopped (It should resemble a salsa more than a soup at this point).
- Move mixture to separate bowl.
- Cube bread into squares.
- Combine bread and oil in the blender.
- Puree until smooth.
- Add to the same bowl with previously mixed vegetables and stir.
- Cover the bowl tightly and set it in the refrigerator for two days.
- Preheat the grill to medium heat.
- Put the scallops on the skewers and season with remaining pepper.
- Cook scallops on the grill until opaque, flipping once.
- Melt butter with lemon zest on the grill in a saucepan.
- Brush scallops with butter mixture.
- Serve gazpacho in bowls.
- Serve skewers over gazpacho and enjoy!

Nutritional Information per serving Calories: 313 Fat: 14 g Carbohydrates: 24 g Protein: 21 g

Garlic Grilled Shrimp

Servings: 8 skewers **Serving size: 1 skewer**

Ingredients
- 1 lb. shrimp, peeled and deveined
- For the marinade
- 4 cloves garlic minced
- ¾ cup olive oil
- 2 tbsps. chopped parsley
- 1 tbsp. fresh basil chopped
- 2 tbsps. lemon juice
- 1 tbsps. tomato paste
- ½ tsp. salt
- ½ tsp. black pepper
- For the Garlic Butter
- 1 clove garlic minced
- ¼ cup butter melted
- 1 tsp. parsley chopped
- lemon wedges for serving (optional)

Directions
- Combine all marinade ingredients in a bowl and whisk. Allow shrimp to marinate at least 20 minutes.
- Preheat the grill to medium heat.
- Thread shrimp on skewers and grill 2-3 minutes per side. Remove from skewers and place in a serving bowl.
- Drizzle with garlic butter and serve warm with lemon wedges if desired and enjoy!

Pans and Ovens

Baked Lemon Salmon with Wild Rice

Servings: 4 servings **Serving size: 1 filet, 8 oz. of rice**

Ingredients
- 4 salmon filets or whole salmon side (cut into fours)
- 2 tbsps. of olive oil
- ½ tsps. of salt to taste
- ¼ tsp. cracked black pepper
- 2 tsps. of minced garlic
- 1 tsp. of italian seasoning
- 2 medium lemons
- For the rice:
- 2 bags of premade/reheatable whole grain or while rice with quinoa
- 2 tsps. of Italian seasoning
- Salt and pepper to taste
- Juice of half a lemon
- 1 tbsp. of salted sweet cream butter and/or olive oil (use both for more flavor)

Directions

For the salmon:
- Preheat the oven to 400° F. Then grease a large baking pan. You may also lay salmon on a pan.
- If you purchased a whole half of salmon, go ahead and slice it up into four. Rub salt and pepper onto the salmon filets.
- Stir together the olive oil, Italian seasoning, garlic, and the juice of half of a lemon into a small bowl. Then spoon the mixtures over the filets after setting them into the greased pan.
- Slice the remainder of the lemon and set the slices on top of the salmon filets, then place the pan into the oven for 15-18 minutes, or maybe longer, based on the thickness of your salmon.

For the rice:
- Grab a skillet and grease with butter and/or olive oil, setting the burner to medium-high heat.
- Press the bags of rice so it is not lumpy, then pour the rice into the skillet and begin adding the lemon, Italian seasoning, salt and pepper, and more olive oil or butter as desired.
- Cook the rice for 5-7 minutes or until all ingredients are combined and warm.
- Serve the salmon over the rice and enjoy!

Nutritional Information per serving Calories: 306 Fat: 18 g Carbohydrates: 1 g Protein: 34 g

Chapter 9: Vegetarian and Vegan

Vegetables and Their Role

Vegetables are the most overlooked food source available to people for several reasons. As stated earlier, many people don't know how to cook vegetables deliciously. Most people prefer to simply boil or steam vegetables, which can destroy their flavor. Nonetheless, vegetables aren't just important. They are one of the four groups of food that you need to balance when pursuing this diet, and they have the potential to be just as delicious, if not more so, than animal products. Even if you're not a vegetarian or a vegan in any capacity, you should consider eating some of these dishes. Not only are they a change of pace, but they can also help you balance out consuming recipes that may not have a perfect balance on their own.

This chapter will feature recipes with limited animal products or none whatsoever. The animal products will also not come from any meat of the animals, but products that can be taken from the animals without hurting them or taking their lives. These will include dairy products and eggs, as you saw in other chapters that featured vegetarian dishes. That said, many replacement plant-based products mimic the properties of these foods. If you are a vegan, you can still enjoy these recipes if you buy the replacement products. Still, there will be recipes in this chapter with no animal products, so seeking substitutes for those won't be necessary.

The caveat with vegetable dishes is that they are best consumed fresh, as they spoil faster than animal products both in storage and as leftovers. Pay close attention to the freshness of the vegetables you use for your meals before preparation and the state of your leftovers, to avoid spoiling or consuming foods that could make you sick. With that said, look over the vegetable and vegan recipes for the best-tasting dishes in your Macro diet journey!

Shopping List

- Eggplants
- Onion
- Cabbage
- Green beans
- Bell peppers
- Low sodium diced tomatoes
- 6 cups canned tomato sauce
- 2 tablespoons tomato paste
- 2 bay leaves
- Thyme
- Basil
- Carrots
- Broccoli florets
- Zucchini
- Olive oil
- Red bells peppers
- Yellow bell peppers
- Garlic
- Canned tomato sauce
- Brown rice
- Cumin
- Salt
- Sugar
- Crushed red pepper flakes
- Black pepper

Eggplant and Rice Stew

Servings: 12 servings

Serving size: 28 oz. of stew, half a cup of rice.

Ingredients
- 2 large eggplants
- 6 tbsps. olive oil
- 2 red or yellow bell peppers, or one of each.
- 4 cloves of garlic
- 15 oz. canned tomato sauce
- Vegan 'beef' broth
- 3 cups brown rice
- 7 cups of water
- 1 tsp. of cumin
- 1 tsp. of salt
- 1 tsp. sugar
- ½ tsp. crushed red pepper flakes
- ¼ tsp. black pepper

Directions
- Preheat a saucepan and large pot to low heat.
- Peel the eggplants, removing the skins and green stems.
- Cut the eggplant into bite-size pieces.
- Seed and cut the peppers into small pieces.
- Mince the garlic cloves.
- Add olive oil and eggplants to the plant and cook for ten minutes. You may need to do this in increments. Repeat with the bell peppers, adding in the onions during the last two minutes with the bell peppers.
- Transfer the eggplant and peppers to the large pot when finished cooking.
- In a separate large bowl, mix the tomato sauce, one cup of water, cumin, salt, sugar, crushed red pepper flakes and black pepper until fully integrated.
- Put the mix in the bowl into the pot and bring to a boil.
- Reduce heat to medium-low and partially cover to allow venting. Simmer for one hour.
- Wash and rinse the rice and add the remaining water to another pot.
- Bring the rice pot to a boil then lower the heat to a simmer. Simmer for 45 minutes, or until the rice has fully absorbed the water.
- Serve stew over rice in a bowl and enjoy!

Nutritional Information per serving Calories: 137 Fat: 7.3 g Carbohydrates: 16 g Protein: 1.8 g

Hearty Vegetable Stew

Servings: 8 servings **Serving size: ⅛ of a serving**

Ingredients
- 1 small onion diced
- 2 cloves garlic minced
- 1 cup carrots diced
- 4 cups of cabbage chopped, approx. ¼ head of cabbage
- 1 cup green beans 1" pieces
- 2 whole bell peppers chopped
- 28 oz. low sodium diced tomatoes
- 6 cups vegan "beef" broth
- 2 tbsps. tomato paste
- 2 bay leaves
- ½ tsp. each thyme & basil
- Pepper to taste
- 2 cups broccoli florets
- 2 cups zucchini sliced

Directions
1. In a large pot cook onion and garlic over medium heat until slightly softened.
2. Add carrots, cabbage and green beans and cook for an additional 5 minutes.
3. Stir in bell peppers, undrained tomatoes, broth, tomato paste, bay leaves, and seasonings. Simmer for 6-7 minutes.
4. Add in zucchini and broccoli. Simmer for an additional 5 minutes or until softened.
5. Remove bay leaves before serving and enjoy!

Nutritional Information per serving Calories: 41 Fat: 0 g Carbohydrates: 7 g Protein: 3 g

Vegan Stew

Servings: 8 servings **Serving size: ⅛ of a serving**

Ingredients
- 9 tbsps. olive oil, divided
- 4 leeks washed, trimmed and sliced (white part only)
- ½ large yellow onion, quartered
- 4 large carrots sliced ½ in. thick
- 3 stalks of celery sliced ½ in. thick
- 4 cloves garlic, minced
- 2 tsps. fresh thyme or ½ tsp. dried
- 1 tsp. fresh rosemary or ½ tsp. dried
- 2 dried bay leaves
- 1 lb. white or cremini mushrooms, halved if large
- 1 lb. turnips or rutabaga cut into ¾ inch cubes
- 1 lb. russet potatoes cut into 3/4 inch cubes
- 1½ cups dry white wine *see note
- 3 tbsps. vegan Worcestershire sauce or regular if not vegan
- 3 tbsps. flour
- 2 cups vegetable broth hot
- 2 tbsps. white wine vinegar
- 3 tbsps. molasses
- 3 tsps. paprika
- Dash hot sauce such as Tabasco
- Salt and pepper to taste
- Chopped parsley (optional) for garnish

Directions
- In a large heavy pot or Dutch oven, heat 6 tablespoons of olive oil over medium heat. Add the sliced leeks and cook until softened, about 5 minutes.
- Put the onions, carrots, celery, garlic, thyme, rosemary, and bay leaves into the pot. Cook, stirring occasionally, until the leeks start to brown.
- Add the mushrooms and turnips or rutabaga. Pour in the wine and Worcestershire sauce and reduce the heat to low. Stir in the potatoes and cover the pot.
- To make the roux, heat the broth in a measuring cup in the microwave until hot. Heat 3 tablespoons of olive oil in a medium saucepan over medium heat. Add in the flour and cook, whisking constantly, until the roux starts to darken, about 4-5 minutes. Gradually add the hot broth while whisking. Add the vinegar, molasses paprika and a dash of tabasco and whisk until smooth. Stir the roux into the stew.
- Simmer the stew, uncovered, until all the vegetables are tender, about 1 hour. If you feel the liquid is evaporating too quickly, you can cover it for a while. Season to taste with salt and pepper. Serve with mashed potatoes or crusty bread and sprinkle with parsley and enjoy!

Nutritional Information per serving Calories: 367 Fat: 16 g Carbohydrates: 40 g Protein: 5 g

Vegan Beef Stew

Servings: 10 cups **Serving size: 2 cups**

Ingredients

- 1 medium yellow or sweet onion
- 4-5 cloves garlic, minced (more or less to taste)
- ½ lb. carrots, diced
- 1½ lbs. potatoes, diced (peel if you wish)
- 1 lb. cremini or white button mushrooms, halved or quartered (omit if you dislike)
- 2 cups diced or torn vegan "beef" like my Beef Seitan (see note 1)
- 3-4 cups vegan "beef" broth (see note 2)
- 1 cup dry red wine (see note 3, can replace with broth)
- 2 tbsps. balsamic vinegar
- 1 tsp. dried thyme
- 1 tsp. smoked paprika
- 1 tsp. agave, optional
- 1 cup lentils, optional (if using, add 2 additional cups broth)

Directions

- If you're using my instant pot seitan (whether you use a pressure cooker or stovetop, instructions for both are included), make it before you start the soup and let it rest for 10 minutes before cubing the amount you'd like to use. I used about half of it for this recipe and kept half for stir-fries.
- Similarly, if you would like to make my vegan Irish soda bread to go with this, make it and let it cool for an hour before slicing to eat with this soup.
- First, let's sauté the onions in a large nonstick pot over medium high heat. Stir the onions frequently and cook for about 3-4 minutes or until translucent. If you cook with oil, you may start with that (I'd use a neutral flavored oil, not olive or coconut). Personally, I cook with water, so I just add a splash of water (about a tablespoon) whenever the onions start to stick.
- Next add the garlic and sauté for another minute.
- Then add the mushrooms. Sauté for another 3 minutes.
- Now add the carrots, potatoes, and herbs and spices and stir.
- Add the vegan seitan chunks (if using) and red wine (if using) to deglaze the pot. Stir again. Note, if you're using tofu, I'd add it once the potatoes and carrots are almost cooked through. If adding lentils, add them now (don't forget the extra broth to compensate; 2 cups broth per 1 cup lentils).
- Add broth, agave, and balsamic vinegar, cover and set the heat to medium. Cook covered for 15-20 minutes, or until potatoes and carrots are fork tender.
- Adjust flavors if needed and remove from heat.
- Serve with vegan Irish soda bread or a crusty French bread and enjoy!

Note: You can refrigerate leftover stew in an airtight container for up to 5 days or freeze in a freezer-safe container for up to 3 months.

Nutritional Information per serving Calories: 371 Fat: 11/2 g Carbohydrates: 43 g Protein: 43.7 g

Chapter 10: Pizzas and Pasta

Italian Delights

Pizza and pasta are comfort foods for many people. Not only are they simple to make and prepare at home, but they're also associated with fine dining, casual eating, and an overall laid back and romantic setting for those enjoying these recipes. They also come from Italy, which is home to the Mediterranean diet. The Mediterranean diet differs from the Macro diet because the former is more of a cultural diet. In contrast, the Macro diet is one based on science. Regardless, both diets show great fitness and life expectancy rates for the people eating them. As you're following the Macro diet, it's best to incorporate elements of the Mediterranean diet into your program because it focuses on vegetables and seafood.

That said, pizza, especially, has an unsavory reputation as a fast-food staple, especially in the United States. This is unfair to pizza's reputation, as it can be made with ingredients to make it more sensible for the Macro diet. It's also important to note that pasta can have the same issues as pizza, if not more, considering its reputation as fast carbohydrates and association with saturated fats. It is important to note the ingredients when making these recipes because they can differentiate between a macro-friendly meal and a meal item at a fast-food restaurant. It's also worth noting that some dishes have no dairy products to avoid the saturated fat content.

Making Your Own Dough?

Both pizza and pasta require making dough or buying premade dough or pasta shapes. That said, making your own dough for both dishes is a good idea because it allows you more control over the food that you want to make. If you are not making your own dough, pay attention to the nutrition facts when buying premade dough and pasta shapes and find the ones that best fit your macro balance. The alternative is to portion yourself to maintain the best possible balance for your macros. As always, it's best to avoid refined grain doughs and pasta shapes made with those grains and look for whole-grain alternatives. This may not always be possible, considering what's available around you. Still, it's best to look for them regardless or see how you can make your own dough from whole grains. This is also important for those with Celiac disease. Many premade doughs and pasta shapes can have gluten in them, so the recipes for the pasta and pizza doughs will purposefully avoid gluten while maintaining macro balancing.

Chapter 11: Snacks

Snacking and Timing

Snacks are a matter of contention for many people. Some say it's a bad idea to eat between meals, whereas others claim it's the best way to stop hunger cravings between meals, so you don't overeat when the next meal comes along. There is wisdom in both statements, but ultimately, snacking comes down to timing and balance. If you eat a lighter breakfast, a snack can help tide you over until it's time for lunch. Suppose you also see that you won't be eating until later than you usually do. In that case, snacks can help maintain your metabolism and keep your balance strong.

It's also important to not overdo it with snacks. Just as eating multiple servings of food is a bad idea for dieters, eating too many snacks is equally as bad. This is why timing is critical for snacks. It's acceptable to have one snack a day in your time between meals if those times are particularly long, but it's not a good idea to eat breakfast at 8:00 A.M. and snack when your next meal is at noon. The snacks in this cookbook are great for those long stretches and for maintaining a healthy balance.

There is also a section dedicated to sweet snacks. These should be enjoyed sparingly or on "cheat days" to ensure the best possible balance. They're included for those looking for a way to indulge during the day. They are an excellent alternative to a dessert dish in a day if a dessert isn't eaten for the rest of the day. So long as you keep your timing right, you'll be good to go with these great snacks!

Shopping List

- Genoa salami
- Provolone cheese
- Lower-sodium roast beef
- Cheddar cheese
- Carrots
- Hummus
- Cucumber
- Deli turkey
- Tuna spread
- Whole wheat crackers
- Eggs
- Apples
- Swiss cheese
- Low sodium ham
- Garbanzo beans
- Olive oil
- Garlic
- Salt
- No sugar added peanut butter
- Celery stalks
- Strawberries
- Unsalted nuts
- Lemon juice
- Pineapple juice
- Chopped watermelon
- Feta cheese
- 1 tbsp. red chili flakes
- Low sodium turkey
- Mango
- Canned artichokes
- Dried Italian seasoning
- Oregano
- Dried chili flakes
- Red onion, diced
- Cilantro stalks
- Jalapeno
- Lime
- Cinnamon oat pancake mix
- Sugar
- Butter
- Blueberries
- Cooking spray
- Eggplants
- Tahini
- Lemon juice
- Smoked paprika
- Yellow onion
- Mayonnaise
- Shredded mozzarella cheese
- Onion powder
- Hot sauce
- Cream cheese
- Greek yogurt
- Parmesan cheese
- Frozen spinach
- Jar of marinated artichoke quarters
- Pineapple
- Low fat yogurt
- Raspberries
- Creamed coconut
- Shredded unsweetened coconut
- Unsweetened Coconut Milk
- Unsweetened Coconut Cream
- Unsweetened Coconut Water
- Shredded Coconut
- Brown sugar
- Vanilla extract
- Instant oatmeal
- Semi-sweet chocolate chips
- Mandarin oranges
- Peach slices
- Maraschino cherries
- Fresh green grapes
- Mini marshmallows
- Diced crystalized ginger
- Sour cream
- 4 oz. Cool Whip
- Vanilla protein powder
- Dry oats
- Sugar-free strawberry gelatin
- Chocolate protein powder
- Dark chocolate chips
- Coconut oil (melted)
- Cocoa powder
- Almond butter
- Skim milk
- Coconut flour
- Almond flour
- Medjool dates
- Raw walnuts
- Cinnamon
- Ground ginger
- Ground nutmeg
- Whole wheat pretzels
- Frozen yogurt
- Old fashioned whole oats
- Honey
- Apple butter
- Banana
- Dried cranberries
- Pumpkin seeds
- Raisins
- Baking soda
- Baking powder
- Protein powder

Protein-Packed

Salami and Provolone Cheese Rolls (Protein)

Servings: 5 servings **Serving size: One roll**

Ingredients
- 5 slices Genoa salami
- 5 slices provolone cheese

Directions
- Place cheese slices in salami slices and roll, tucking to maintain shape.
- Serve and enjoy!

Nutritional Information per serving Calories: 217 Fat: 17.8 g Carbohydrates: 0.9 g Protein: 13.2 g

Roast Beef and Cheddar Cheese Rolls (Protein)

Servings: 5 servings **Serving size: One roll**

Ingredients
- 5 slices lower sodium roast beef
- 5 slices cheddar cheese

Directions
- Place cheese slices in roast beef slices and roll, tucking to maintain shape.
- Serve and enjoy!

Nutritional Information per serving Calories: 271 Fat: 14.6 g Carbohydrates: 0.4 g Protein: 32.8 g

Sliced Carrots and Hummus

Servings: 4 servings **Serving size: 1/4 of carrot and one tbsp. of hummus**

Ingredients
- 1 large carrot
- 4 tbsps. Hummus

Directions
- Wash the carrot thoroughly and remove the stem, including the brown part.
- Chop into bite-size pieces.
- Serve with hummus and enjoy!

Nutritional Information per serving Calories: 32 Fat: 1.4 g Carbohydrates: 3.9 g Protein: 1.4 g

Cucumber Turkey Sliders

Servings: 4 servings **Serving size: One slider**

Ingredients
- 1 cucumber
- 4 slices deli turkey
- 4 slices cheddar cheese

Directions
- Peel and cut the cucumber into eight slices
- Fold the turkey and cheese in between two cucumber slices, using toothpicks to hold in place if needed.
- Serve and enjoy!

Nutritional Information per serving Calories: 194 Fat: 11.9 g Carbohydrates: 3.9 g Protein: 17.1/2 g

Whole Wheat Tuna Crackers

Servings: 8 servings

Serving size: Two crackers, 3 oz. tuna spread per cracker, three slices of cucumbers per cracker.

Ingredients
- 1 cucumber
- 24 oz. tuna spread
- 8 whole wheat crackers

Directions
- Wash the cucumber and cut it into thin slices.
- Spread the tuna over the crackers.
- Add the cucumber slices and enjoy!

Nutritional Information per serving Calories: 66 Fat: 3.4 g Carbohydrates: 6.7 g Protein: 2.9 g

Hard-Boiled Eggs with Apples and Carrots

Servings: 3 servings

Ingredients
- 6 eggs
- 1 apple
- 1 carrot

Directions
- Preheat a saucepan with enough water to cover the eggs and bring to a boil.
- Clean and slice the apple and carrot to bite-size pieces.
- Add the eggs to the water and cover for 9-12 minutes.
- Gently remove the egg shells.

Whole Wheat Turkey Crackers

Servings: 3 servings

Serving size: Two crackers, one slice of turkey per cracker, one slice of cheese per cracker.

Ingredients
- 6 whole wheat crackers
- 6 slices deli turkey
- 6 slices cheddar cheese

Directions
- Place one slice of cheese and turkey per cracker.
- Serve and enjoy!

Nutritional Information per serving Calories: 184 Fat: 11.4 g Carbohydrates: 6.8 g Protein: 13.8 g

Whole Wheat Roast Beef Crackers

Servings: 3 servings

Serving size: Two crackers, one slice of turkey per cracker, one slice of cheese per cracker.

Ingredients
- 6 whole wheat crackers
- 6 slices roast beef
- 6 slices Swiss cheese

Directions
- Place one slice of cheese and roast beef per cracker.
- Serve and enjoy!

Nutritional Information per serving Calories: 282 Fat: 13.8 g Carbohydrates: 4.3 g Protein: 33.7 g

Ham and Cheese Rolls

Servings: 6 servings

Serving size: One slice of ham, one slice of cheese.

Ingredients
- 6 slices low sodium ham
- 6 slices cheddar cheese

Directions
- Place the slices of cheese into the slices of ham, tucking to maintain shape.
- Serve and enjoy!

Nutritional Information per serving Calories: 173 Fat: 10.3 g Carbohydrates: 2.4 g Protein: 17 g

Cucumber Ham Sliders

Servings: 4 servings

Serving size: Two slices of cucumbers, one slice of ham, one slice of cheese.

Ingredients
- 1 cucumber
- 4 slices low sodium ham
- 4 slices cheddar cheese

Directions
- Peel and cut the cucumber into eight slices
- Fold the ham and cheese in between two cucumber slices, using toothpicks to hold in place if needed.
- Serve and enjoy!

Nutritional Information per serving Calories: 184 Fat: 10.4 g Carbohydrates: 5.1 g Protein: 17.1/2 g

Cucumber Roast Beef Sliders

Servings: 4 servings

Serving size: Two slices of cucumbers, one slice of roast beef, one slice of cheese.

Ingredients
- 1 cucumber
- 4 slices low sodium ham
- 4 slices cheddar cheese

Directions
- Peel and cut the cucumber into eight slices.
- Fold the roast beef and cheese in between two cucumber slices, using toothpicks to hold in place if needed.
- Serve and enjoy!

Nutritional Information per serving Calories: 191 Fat: 9.1 g Carbohydrates: 2.7 g Protein: 24.1/2 g

Whole Wheat Ham Crackers

Servings: 6 servings

Serving size: One cracker, one slice of ham, and one slice of cheese.

Ingredients
- 6 whole wheat crackers
- 6 slices low sodium ham
- 6 slices cheddar cheese

Directions
- Place one slice of cheese and ham per cracker.
- Serve and enjoy!

Nutritional Information per serving Calories: 191 Fat: 11 g Carbohydrates: 5.1 g Protein: 17.3 g

Garlic Garbanzo Beans

Servings: 4 servings **Serving size: 1/2 cup of total mixture.**

Ingredients
- 2 cups garbanzo beans
- 2 tbsps. olive oil
- 1 clove garlic
- Salt to taste

Directions
- Rinse the garbanzo beans in water for 24 hours. Drain, then move to a large bowl.
- Mince the garlic clove.
- Mix the garlic clove, garbanzo beans, and olive oil in the large bowl. Add salt to taste as desired.
- Serve and enjoy!

Nutritional Information per serving Calories: 425 Fat: 13 g Carbohydrates: 60.9 g Protein: 19.4 g

Fruits and Veggies

Sliced Apple and Peanut Butter

Servings: One serving

Ingredients
- 1 apple
- 1 tbsp. no sugar added peanut butter

Directions
- Core and cut the apple into slices.
- Serve with peanut butter to dip or spread and enjoy!

Nutritional Information per serving Calories: 495 Fat: 16.4 g Carbohydrates: 42.4 g Protein: 30.2 g

Peanut Butter and Strawberry Celery Sticks

Servings: One serving

Serving size: 1 tbsp. of peanut butter's worth of celery sticks and strawberries.

Ingredients
- 1 celery stalk
- 2 tbsps. peanut butter
- 1 cup strawberries

Directions Wash and chop the celery to bite-size portions.
Wash and quarter the strawberries, removing the leaves.
Spread the peanut butter over the celery, topping it with strawberries.

Nutritional Information per serving Calories: 106 Fat: 8.2 g Carbohydrates: 6.1 g Protein: 4.3 g

Dried Apples with Nuts

Servings: 2 **Serving size: Half a cup of nuts, and half an apple**

Ingredients
- 1 apple
- 1 cup unsalted nuts, no salt added.
- 1 tbsp. lemon juice
- 1 cup pineapple juice
- 1 tbsp. of water

Directions Preheat the oven or toaster oven to 145° F.
Mix the juices and water in a bowl, stirring to maintain consistency.
Wash, core, and slice the apples into thin rings.
Dip the apple slices into the mix and spread evenly across a baking tray with parchment paper.
Bake for 10-20 hours with the oven door open, removing apples when uneven curls appear.
Serve with mixed nuts in a bowl and enjoy!

Nutritional Information per serving Calories: 533 Fat: 35.7 g Carbohydrates: 49 g Protein: 12.7 g

Spicy Watermelon and Feta Cheese

Servings: 2 **Serving size: Half a cup of nuts, and half an apple (91 g)**

Ingredients
- 2 cups chopped watermelon
- 1 cup feta cheese
- 1 tbsp. olive oil
- 1 tbsp. red chili flakes

Directions Spread the feta cheese, olive oil, and chili flakes over the watermelon as desired.

Nutritional Information per serving Calories: 152 Fat: 11.6 g Carbohydrates: 7.2 g Protein: 5.8 g

Mango Wrapped in Turkey

Servings: 3
Serving size: One slice of turkey, one third of mango (50 g)

Ingredients
- 3 slices low-sodium turkey
- 1 mango

Directions Wash, peel and slice the mango into thirds, removing the skin and seeds.
Wrap turkey slices around mango thirds and enjoy!

Nutritional Information per serving Calories: 127 Fat: 0.9 g Carbohydrates: 16.8 g Protein: 12.9 g

Marinated Artichoke Hearts

Servings: 4
Serving size: Roughly 100 grams of artichoke hearts

Ingredients
- 14 oz. can artichokes canned in water (397g)
- 1-2 cloves garlic sliced thin
- 1 tsp. dried Italian seasoning or oregano
- 1 tsp. grounded black pepper
- ½ tsp. dried chili flakes
- ½ tsp. salt or to taste
- ⅔ cup olive oil
- ¼ cup fresh lemon juice

Directions Drain the artichoke hearts and rinse them in water, placing them into jars
Add all other ingredients to the jar and shake lightly to mix.
Serve immediately or keep up to three weeks refrigerated and enjoy!

Nutritional Information per serving Calories: 202 Fat: 20.3 g Carbohydrates: 6.3 g Protein: 1 g

Cucumbers with Mango Salsa

Servings: 3
Serving size: 33 g of cucumber dipped in sauce.

Ingredients
- 2 cucumbers, peeled and sliced to chip size
- 1 red onion, diced
- 1 mango, peeled, seed removed, and diced
- 1 bunch of cilantro stalks, finely chopped
- 1 jalapeno chopped
- 1 tsp. freshly squeezed lime juice (not bottled)

Directions Mix all ingredients except cucumbers in a bowl and stir until blended.
Serve and enjoy!

Nutritional Information per serving Calories: 124 Fat: 0.7 g Carbohydrates: 29.8 g Protein: 3.7 g

Macro Blueberry Crisp

Servings: 6
Serving size: One sixth of total crisp

Ingredients
- 1 cup cinnamon oat pancake mix
- 4 tsps. sugar
- 3 tbsps. melted butter
- 3 cups frozen Blueberries
- Cooking Spray

Directions Preheat the oven to 350° F.
Spray an 8x8 in. casserole plate with cooking spray.
Stir cake mix and melted butter in a bowl until crumbles form and set aside.
Mix blueberries and sugar in a separate bowl and place in the casserole plate.
Add the crumbles on top of the blueberries, making sure to break apart larger crumbles and spread through the top.

Bake for 25 minutes.
Let it cool, serve, and enjoy!

Nutritional Information per serving Calories: 190 Fat: 7 g Carbohydrates: 26.7 g Protein: 7 g

Sliced Pears and Almond Butter

Servings: 1

Ingredients
- 1 pear
- 1 tbsp. no sugar added almond butter

Directions Wash the pear and slice it to desired shapes.
Serve with almond butter as a dip and enjoy!

Nutritional Information per serving Calories: 170 Fat: 20.3 g Carbohydrates: 24.7 g Protein: 1 g

Baba Ghanouj and Whole Wheat Crackers

Servings: 4 **Serving size: 4 crackers dipped in baba ghanouj**

Ingredients
- 16 whole wheat crackers
- 2 medium eggplants
- ¼ cup tahini
- 3 tbsps. fresh lemon juice
- 2 tbsps. extra virgin olive oil
- 2 garlic cloves
- ½ tsp. sea salt
- 1 dash smoked paprika

Directions Preheat oven to 400º F.
Puncture the eggplants in various places with a fork to prevent exploding while baking.
Wrap the eggplant in foil.
Bake for 40-50 minutes.
Once the eggplant is cool, remove the skin and halve, removing all the seeds.
Place the eggplant in a strainer pot and set with water for 20 minutes.
Place all the ingredients except the cucumber in a blender and puree until smooth.
Serve with crackers and enjoy!

Nutritional Information per serving Calories: 283 Fat: 18.3 g Carbohydrates: 28.4 g Protein: 6.4 g

Carrots and Caramelized Onion Dip

Servings: 12 **Serving size: 10 grams of carrot slices with dip**

Ingredients
- 2 carrots
- 1 yellow onion
- ½ cup of mayonnaise
- 2 cups shredded mozzarella cheese
- 1 tbsp. butter
- 1 tsp. onion powder
- 1 tbsp. hot sauce

Directions Preheat the pan to medium heat.
Dice the onion to a small ring size.
Preheat the oven to 350º F.
Sauté the onions in butter until caramelized.
In a medium oven-safe bowl, add the rest of the ingredients except the carrots, adding the onions when they're done caramelizing.
Bake for 25-30 minutes. Wash and slice the carrots to chip size.

Nutritional Information per serving Calories: 135 Fat: 11.7 g Carbohydrates: 5.1 g Protein: 3.1 g

Whole Wheat Crackers and Artichoke Dip

Servings: 12 **Serving size: three crackers with dip**

Ingredients
- 36 whole wheat crackers
- 12 oz. cream cheese
- 1 cup Greek yogurt
- ¾ cup Parmesan cheese
- 6 cloves garlic, minced
- 30 oz. frozen spinach, thawed and drained of moisture
- 30 oz. jar marinated artichoke quarters, drained and coarsely chopped
- ¾ cup shredded mozzarella cheese

Directions Preheat oven to 375° F.
In a hand mixer, mix together the cream cheese, Greek yogurt, Parmesan cheese, and garlic cloves.
Remove the mix from the mixer and transfer to an oven-safe bowl.
Add the spinach and artichokes to the mix, stirring to keep consistency.
Top with mozzarella cheese and bake for 20-30 minutes, until the cheese is brown.
Serve hot with crackers and enjoy!

Nutritional Information per serving Calories: 352 Fat: 18.3 g Carbohydrates: 24.7 g Protein: 25.9 g

Sweets

Frozen Pineapple and Yogurt Rings

Servings: 8 **Serving size: Half a cup of rings**

Ingredients
- 1 pineapple (4½ cups)
- 1 quart of low-fat yogurt.

Directions Prepare a baking tray with parchment paper.
Wash and peel the pineapple, removing the skin and leaves on top.
Cut the pineapple into 1/2-in. thick slices and dip in yogurt, spreading them over the tray.
Let chill in the freezer until yogurt is solid.
Serve and enjoy!

Nutritional Information per serving Calories: 123 Fat: 0.1 g Carbohydrates: 25.4 g Protein: 4 g

Coconut Stuffed Raspberries

Servings: 4 **Serving size: Five raspberries**

Ingredients
- 2 cups raspberries
- ½ cup creamed coconut
- ¼ cup shredded unsweetened coconut

Directions Wash the raspberries thoroughly, holding them upside down to remove any remaining water.
Place the raspberries in a small muffin tin or other small container to keep them upright.
Ensure the coconut cream is pliable and soft by warming it in plastic with hot water.
Pour the coconut cream into each raspberry tin, being careful not to overfill them.
Sprinkle shredded coconut over the raspberries.
Serve and enjoy!

Nutritional Information per serving Calories: 123 Fat: 9.3 g Carbohydrates: 11.7 g Protein: 1.8 g

Frozen Coconut Sorbet

Servings: 12   **Serving size: 1/12 of total sorbet**

Ingredients
- 2 (13.66 oz.) cans unsweetened coconut milk
- 1 (13.66 oz.) can unsweetened coconut cream
- 8 oz. unsweetened coconut water
- 1 cup granulated sugar, adjust to taste
- ⅔ cup shredded coconut, optional

Directions (This recipe requires an Ice Cream maker)
- Preheat a saucepan to low heat.
- Pour the coconut water and sugar into the pan, stirring until the sugar dissolves.
- Transfer coconut water to the refrigerator until it cools completely.
- Place the coconut water and the coconut cream in a blender and blend until fully mixed.
- Pour the contents of the blender into the ice cream maker and churn until it reaches soft serve consistency.
- Mix in the shredded coconut as the consistency is reached and transfer contents to a freezer-safe container, freezing for at least three hours.
- Serve and enjoy!

Nutritional Information per serving Calories: 385 Fat: 22.4 g Carbohydrates: 48.6 g Protein: 2 g

Chocolate Oat Bars

Servings: 32   **Serving size: one bar**

Ingredients
- 1 cup of butter
- Cooking spray for the pan
- ½ cup packed brown sugar
- 1 tsp. vanilla extract
- 3 cups instant oatmeal
- 1 cup semisweet chocolate chips
- ½ cup no sugar added peanut butter

Directions Preheat a cooking pan over medium heat.
Use the cooking spray for a 9x9 in. cooking tray.
Melt the butter in the pan and mix in brown sugar and vanilla.
Add in the oats and cook over low heat for two to three minutes until the ingredients are mixed.
Pour the mixture into the cooking tray, evenly distributing and pressing down.
In a pan over low heat, melt and mix the peanut butter and chocolate chips. Stir until smooth.
Pour the mixture over the oats in the tray, spreading evenly.
Let the cooking tray refrigerate for 2 to 3 hours, or overnight, if possible.
Cut into 32 even bars and enjoy!

Nutritional Information per serving Calories: 38g Fat: 22.4 g Carbohydrates: 48.6 g Protein: 2 g

Classic Ambrosia

Servings: 12   **Serving size: 1/2 cup**

Ingredients
- 15 oz. can mandarin oranges
- 15 oz. can peach slices, drained
- 8 oz. can chopped pineapple
- 5 oz. jar maraschino cherries, stems removing the stems
- ¾ cup fresh green grapes, halved lengthwise
- ¾ cup sweetened coconut flakes
- ¾ cup mini marshmallows
- ¼ cup diced crystalized ginger
- 4 oz. sour cream
- 4 oz. cool whip
- A pinch of salt

Directions Thoroughly wash all the fruit.
Prepare a large colander in your sink.
Pour the oranges, peaches, pineapple bits and cherries into the colander.
Once the peaches are drained properly, slice them into 3-4 pieces.
Cut the cherries and grapes in half, making sure they have no stems or branches.
Dice the ginger finely, then put all the ingredients in a large salad bowl and mix gently with a wooden spoon.
Serve and enjoy!

Nutritional Information per serving Calories: 172 Fat: 7 g Carbohydrates: 27 g Protein: 2 g

Strawberry Cake Balls

Servings: 6   **Serving size: 1 ball**

Ingredients
- 1 scoop (30 g) vanilla protein powder
- ¾ cup oats, dry
- 1 tbsp. sugar free gelatin powder, strawberry flavor
- ½ cup of strawberries, not frozen

Directions
- Put the oats, protein powder, and gelatin powder in a blender.
- Add in half a strawberry and blend, the goal is to get a dough-like consistency. Adding too many strawberries will turn it into mush, too little, and it will be powdery. Add more ingredients as needed to reach intended consistency.
- Once the dough reaches cake-like consistency, roll it up into six individual balls and enjoy!

Nutritional Information per serving Calories: 31 Fat: 0.1 g Carbohydrates: 27 g Protein: 5.7 g

Chocolate and Coconut Protein Balls

Servings: 8   **Serving size: 1 ball**

Ingredients
- 3 scoops (90 g) chocolate protein powder
- ¾ cup dark chocolate chips
- ½ tbsp. coconut oil, melted
- ¾ cup cocoa powder
- ½ cup unsweetened shredded coconut
- 2 tbsps. almond butter
- 2–4 tbsps. skim milk
- 1 pinch of salt

Directions
- Melt the coconut oil and chocolate chips in a microwave-safe bowl for one minute. Stir, then microwave again for 30 more seconds, or until butter is fully melted.
- In a different bowl, add the protein powder, cocoa powder, shredded coconut, and salt. Mix until fully integrated.
- Add the melted ingredients to the dry ones. Stir persistently, as it may be difficult for the mix to come together.
- Add the milk and continue mixing. Use more milk as needed if the dough is too hard.
- Roll into nine separate balls and refrigerate for ten minutes.

Nutritional Information per serving Calories: 136 Fat: 7 g Carbohydrates: 9.3 g Protein: 12.3 g

Carrot Cake Balls

Servings: 16   **Serving size: 1 ball**

Ingredients

- 4-6 tbsp. coconut flour or almond flour
- ¾ cup shredded carrot
- 1 cup packed pitted Medjool dates
- 1¾ cups raw walnuts or other nut of choice
- 2 tsps. vanilla extract
- ¼ tsp. sea salt
- ¾ tsp. ground cinnamon
- ½ tsp. ground ginger
- 1 pinch of ground nutmeg

Directions

- Grate the carrot and set aside.
- Remove the pits from the dates and add them to the blender.
- Blend until a ball shape forms. Set it aside.
- Blend nuts, vanilla, salt, and spices together for 15 seconds until a semi-fine powder is achieved.
- Add the carrots and dates to the blender, pulsing until a loose dough forms and carrots are still visible.
- Add the coconut powder and pulse more, stirring in between pulses to achieve a dough consistency.
- Roll the dough into balls, using more almond or coconut powder if they're sticky.
- Place the balls in the freezer for 10-15 minutes, then serve and enjoy!

Nutritional Information per serving Calories: 142 Fat: 5.4 g Carbohydrates: 24.1 g Protein: 2 g

Frozen Yogurt Pretzels

Servings: 5 **Serving size: Five pretzels and 1/4 cup of yogurt**

Ingredients

- 1 cup yogurt
- 20 whole wheat pretzels

Directions Prepare a baking tray with parchment paper.
Dip the pretzels in the yogurt, spreading them over the tray.
Let chill in the freezer until yogurt is solid.
Serve and enjoy!

Nutritional Information per serving Calories: 310 Fat: 0.1 g Carbohydrates: 27 g Protein: 5.7 g

Frozen Yogurt Apple Slices

Servings: 1

Ingredients

- 1 apple
- 1 cup frozen yogurt

Directions Prepare a baking tray with parchment paper.
Wash and core the apple, removing the stem and seeds.
Cut the apple into ½-in. thick slices and dip in yogurt, spreading them over the tray.
Let chill in the freezer until yogurt is solid.
Serve and enjoy!

Nutritional Information per serving Calories: 290 Fat: 3.4 g Carbohydrates: 48.1 g Protein: 14.6 g

Breakfast Oatmeal Cookies

Servings: 12 cookies **Serving size: One cookie**

Ingredients

- 2 cups old-fashioned whole oats
- ½ tsp. salt
- 1 tsp. ground cinnamon
- 1 cup almond butter
- ¼ cup honey
- ¾ cup apple butter
- 1 large banana, mashed
- ½ cup dried cranberries
- ½ cup pumpkin seeds
- ½ cup raisins

Directions
- Preheat the oven to 325º F.
- Line two baking sheets with parchment paper (or use cooking spray).
- Mix all ingredients in a mixer, making sure the bananas are fully mashed before doing so.
- Continue to mix until a soft, pliable dough consistency is reached.
- Scoop the dough into ¼ cup mounds and place on the baking sheets. Flatten the mounds into cookie shape with the back of the spoon and ensure enough space between the cookies to prevent sticking.
- Bake for 16-18 minutes or until golden brown.
- Let cool for ten minutes and enjoy!

Nutritional Information per serving Calories: 130 Fat: 3.9 g Carbohydrates: 22.9 g Protein: 2.9 g

Banana Protein Muffins

Servings: 12   **Serving size: 1 muffin**

Ingredients
- 3 small-medium bananas (about 1 cup mashed)
- 3 eggs
- 1 tbsp. honey, optional
- 1 tsp. vanilla
- ¾ cup almond flour
- 1 tsp. baking soda
- ½ tsp. baking powder
- A pinch of salt
- ½ tsp. cinnamon
- 2 scoops protein powder
- ¾ cup natural almond butter
- Cooking spray for muffin liners.

Directions
- Preheat the oven to 350º F.
- Spray the muffin tray with the cooking spray.
- In a mixing bowl, mash the bananas until no large chunks remain.
- Add eggs, vanilla, and honey, into the bowl whisking until properly mixed.
- Mix in the almond flour, baking soda, baking powder, salt, and protein powder.
- Mix until the dough reaches proper consistency (solid, but soft).
- Put the batter into the muffin tray slots, about ¾ of the slot should be filled.
- Bake for 15-20 minutes until brown. Test by puncturing muffins with a toothpick and pulling it out. When no dough appears, the muffins are ready.
- Let cool for 20 minutes.

Nutritional Information per serving Calories: 101 Fat: 4.3 g Carbohydrates: 9.7 g Protein: 6.7 g

Chapter 12: Desserts

Delightful Desserts

With all this talk of balance and managing your macros, it may seem strange that this cookbook features a desserts chapter, but there's a good reason for this. Humans naturally seek delicious foods, and refined sugar is among the most addictive substances on the planet. It makes more sense to control your sugar craving than leave it to overtake you. It's also essential to give yourself a break from the diet every now and then to indulge in a dessert that lifts your spirits as you eat it.

That said, these desserts should be eaten sparingly to maintain your macro balance. These are best enjoyed once every other day at most and once a week at best for any "cheat days" you wish to have. Desserts have a large amount of sugar, which causes many issues for anyone looking to lose weight or maintain a healthy body. These recipes try to either minimize refined sugars or focus on natural sugars, which is the best way to approach desserts even if you're not pursuing the Macro diet.

The three categories are no coincidence either. The best time to eat desserts is at the beginning of the day, so your body can use its energy to work off the sugar as the day progresses. For this reason, I've included a chapter dedicated to breakfast desserts such as pancakes, crepes, and waffles. The fruit dessert section is there because fruits have nutritional benefits on their own and are the best desserts to eat for those looking to eat dessert more often. Finally, the dairy section is dedicated to genuinely indulgent desserts. These should be eaten the least of the other sections because many traditional desserts are in this section. They can also be the most damaging to your progress in the diet. These desserts are the ones best enjoyed once a week at most.

Shopping List

- Waffle Iron
- Skim milk
- Pumpkin puree
- Eggs
- Vegetable oil
- Vinegar
- All-purpose flour
- Brown sugar
- Baking powder
- Baking soda
- Ground allspice
- Ground cinnamon
- Ground ginger
- Salt
- Cooking spray
- Pumpkin pie spice
- Cinnamon
- Nutmeg
- Ginger
- Butter
- Dark brown sugar
- Cream Cheese
- Heavy Whipping Cream
- Vanilla Extract
- Powdered Sugar
- Whole wheat flour
- Sugar
- Buttermilk
- Honey
- Whole-grain pastry flour
- Plain yogurt
- Banana
- Kiwis
- Old fashioned oats
- Whole milk
- Strawberries
- Blueberries
- Raspberries
- Maple syrup
- Almond milk
- Natural peanut butter
- Frozen blueberries
- Walnuts
- Lemon zest
- Pineapple
- Vanilla Greek yogurt
- Nonfat plain Greek yogurt
- Ancient grain granola
- Mascarpone cheese
- Heavy cream
- No sugar added liquid sweetener
- Olive oil
- Honey
- Protein powder
- Cornstarch
- Pecans
- Almond extract
- Pre-packed wonton
- Premade light cherry pie filling
- Premade raspberry pie filling
- Premade apple pie filling
- Premade blueberry pie filling
- Oats rolled oats or quick cooking
- Raisins
- Flax seeds
- Erythritol or another sugar substitute.
- Macadamia nuts
- Vanilla protein powder
- Greek yogurt cream cheese
- Canned 100% pumpkin
- Sweet potato or yams
- Confectioners' style erythritol
- Ground cloves
- Ground ginger
- Liquid sweetener
- Pitted dates
- Vanilla whey protein powder
- Egg whites
- Graham Crackers
- Unsweetened vanilla almond milk
- Natural butter flavoring
- Evaporated Fat-Free Milk
- Liquid Stevia Extract
- Dried Nonfat Milk
- Powdered Erythritol
- Xanthan Gum
- Egg Yolks
- Organic Corn Starch
- Key Lime Zest
- Key Lime Juice
- Molasses
- Dark chocolate chips
- Glutinous rice flour
- Soy sauce
- Potato starch
- Vanilla wafers
- Light butter
- Cottage cheese
- Sugar free cheesecake pudding mix
- 3 tbsps. no sugar added sweetener
- White chocolate
- No sugar added sweetener
- Wholesome Yum Blanched Almond Flour
- Espresso
- Cocoa powder
- Unsweetened almond milk
- White rice
- Coconut milk
- Birthday Cake Ice Cream
- Peanut Butter protein bar

Breakfast Desserts

Pumpkin Pancakes

Servings: 6   **Serving size: Two pancakes**

Ingredients
- 1½ cups skim milk
- 1 cup pumpkin puree (225 g of pumpkin)
- 1 egg
- 2 tbsps. vegetable oil
- 2 tbsps. vinegar
- 2 cups all-purpose flour
- 3 tbsps. brown sugar
- 2 tsps. baking powder
- 1 tsp. baking soda
- 1 tsp. ground allspice
- 1 tsp. ground cinnamon
- ½ tsp. ground ginger
- ½ tsp. salt
- Cooking spray for the skillet

Directions
- Preheat a skillet to medium-low heat.
- Puree the pumpkin in the blender until smooth.
- Whisk together the rest of the ingredients in a separate bowl, incorporating the pumpkin puree until a batter consistency is achieved.
- Spray the skillet with the cooking spray and make pancakes with ¼ cup of batter. Do not pat the pancakes while cooking to maintain fluffy texture.
- Flip the pancakes when needed and serve with fruits or no sugar added syrup as desired.
- Enjoy!

Nutritional Information per serving Calories: 261 Fat: 5.8 g Carbohydrates: 44.1 g Protein: 7.7 g

Pumpkin Spice Waffles

Servings: 6   **Serving size: Two Waffles**

Ingredients
- 1½ cups all-purpose flour
- 1½ tsp. baking powder
- 1½ tsp. baking soda
- 1 tbsp. pumpkin pie spice or 1 tsp. each of cinnamon, nutmeg, and ginger
- ½ tsp. salt
- 225 g of pumpkin to make puree
- 2 eggs
- 3 tbsps. butter melted
- 1/2 cup dark brown sugar
- 1 cup of skim milk
- Cooking Spray for the waffle iron.

Directions Preheat the waffle iron to medium heat.
Puree the pumpkin in a blender until smooth
Whisk all the ingredients in a large bowl until a batter consistency forms
Spray the waffle iron before each waffle, ¼ cup per waffle.
Serve with fruits or no sugar added syrup as desired and enjoy!

Nutritional Information per serving Calories: 345 Fat: 13 g Carbohydrates: 46 g Protein: 10 g

Pumpkin Crepes with Pumpkin Filling

Servings: 6   **Serving size: One Crepe**

Ingredients

For the Filling:
- 2 ½ tbsps. canned pumpkin
- 8 oz. softened cream cheese
- 2 cups heavy whipping cream

- ½ tsp. vanilla extract
- ¼ cup powdered sugar

For the Crepes:
- 2 eggs
- 1 cup flour
- 1 cup milk
- Pumpkin spice or cinnamon to taste
- ½ cup water
- 1 tsp. salt
- ⅛ cup canned pumpkin
- 2 tbsps. melted butter

Directions

Crepes
- Preheat a skillet pan to medium heat.
- In a blender, blend the pumpkin, milk, water, salt, and eggs until it just reaches consistency.
- Add the flour and blend, use less than listed if necessary, to achieve crepe batter.
- Melt the butter in the skillet pan and add ¼ cups crepe batter at a time per crepe, cooking for 1 to 1½ minutes on each side.

Filling
- Soften the cream cheese by microwaving it for ten seconds on a microwave-safe plate.
- In a mixing bowl, whip the cream until the consistency allows soft peaks to form.
- Add the vanilla and the sugar and whisk in the cream cheese in portions.
- Add the tablespoons of the pumpkin extract and whisk together with the other ingredients in the bowl.
- Serve in two tablespoons per crepe and roll up. Enjoy!

Nutritional Information per serving Calories: 581 Fat: 48 g Carbohydrates: 29 g Protein: 10 g

Whole Wheat Pancakes and Berries

Servings: 3 **Serving size: Three pancakes**

Ingredients
- 1 cup whole wheat flour (5 oz. by weight)
- 2 tsps. sugar
- ½ tsp. baking powder
- ¼ tsp. baking soda
- ¼ tsp. salt
- 1 cup buttermilk
- 1 egg
- 2 tbsps. melted butter
- Cooking Spray for the skillet pan

Directions Preheat a skillet to medium heat.
Whisk together the whole wheat flour, sugar, baking powder, baking soda, and salt in a large bowl.
Melt the butter in the skillet and transfer to a separate bowl.
In another large bowl, whisk the buttermilk, egg, and melted butter.
Preheat a clean skillet pan.
Pour the contents with liquid into the other bowl and whisk until a batter consistency is reached.
Spray the skillet with the cooking spray and make pancakes with ¼ cup of batter for each pancake. Do not pat the pancakes while cooking to maintain fluffy texture.
Flip the pancakes when needed and serve with fruits or no sugar added syrup as desired. Enjoy!

Nutritional Information per serving Calories: 286 Fat: 12 g Carbohydrates: 35 g Protein: 9 g

Whole Wheat Waffles and Cream

Servings: 1 **Serving size: Four waffles**

Ingredients
- 2 eggs
- 1¾ cups skim milk
- ¼ cup butter

- 1 tbsp. honey
- ½ tsp. cinnamon, ground
- ¼ tsp. baking soda
- 1½ cups whole wheat flour
- 2 tsps. baking powder
- ⅛ tsp. salt

Directions Preheat the waffle iron to medium heat.
Whisk together the eggs, milk, butter, honey, cinnamon, and baking soda in a large bowl until mixed well.
Add in the flour, baking powder, and salt and whisk, being careful to avoid lumps by consistently mixing until a batter consistency forms.
Spray the waffle iron before each waffle, using ¼ of a cup of batter per waffle.
Serve with fruits or no sugar added syrup as desired and enjoy!

Nutritional Information per serving Calories: 286 Fat: 12 g Carbohydrates: 35 g Protein: 9 g

Whole Wheat Crepes with Kiwis

Servings: 2   Serving size: One crepe

Ingredients

For the crepes:
- 1 cup whole grain pastry flour
- ¼ tsp. salt
- 1 egg
- 2 cups skim milk
- 1½ tsps. vanilla extract
- 2 tsps. butter
- 2 tbsps. water

For the filling:
- ½ cup plain yogurt
- 1 banana
- 2 kiwis
- ½ tsp. ground cinnamon

Directions

Crepes Preheat a skillet pan to medium heat.
Whisk the egg, flour, milk, and vanilla extract in a large bowl.
Add the flour and whisk, use less than listed if necessary, to achieve crepe batter.
Melt the butter in the skillet pan and add ¼ cup crepe batter at a time per crepe, cooking for 1 to 1½ minutes on each side.

Filling Chop the bananas and kiwis into long slices.
Mix all filling ingredients together in a large bowl.
Serve with one tablespoon of filling per crepe and enjoy!

Nutritional Information per serving Calories: 363 Fat: 7.6 g Carbohydrates: 53 g Protein: 17.3 g

Triple Berry Oatmeal

Servings: 2   Serving size: One 28 oz bowl

Ingredients
- 1 cup old fashioned oats
- 1 cup whole milk
- ¾ cup strawberries
- ¾ cup blueberries
- ¾ cup raspberries
- ¼ tsp. cinnamon
- ¼ tsp. vanilla extract
- 1 tbsp. maple syrup
- A pinch of salt

Directions Preheat a small pot to medium high heat.
Wash all the berries by rinsing them under cold water, removing the stems from the strawberries.
Add the milk, oats, cinnamon, vanilla extract, maple syrup, and salt to the pot and stir until it boils.
Crush the berries with the back of a spoon and add them to the pot.
Lower heat to medium low, cover, and cook for five more minutes.

Nutritional Information per serving Calories: 289 Fat: 6.9 g Carbohydrates: 48 g Protein: 9.9 g

Peanut Butter and Banana Pancakes

Servings: 3   **Serving size: Three pancakes**

Ingredients
- 1 ripe banana
- 1 cup whole wheat flour
- 1 tbsp. baking powder
- ½ tsp. salt
- 1 tsp. cinnamon
- 1 cup almond milk
- 1 tbsp. maple syrup (or more to taste)
- 3 tbsps. natural peanut butter
- 1 cup strawberries

Directions
- Preheat a skillet pan to medium heat.
- Mash the bananas and dice the strawberries.
- Mix the bananas with the milk, syrup, and peanut butter.
- Mix the baking powder, salt, cinnamon, and flour in a separate large bowl.
- Transfer the contents of both bowls into one and mix together. Let it sit for ten minutes once batter consistency is reached.
- Spray the skillet with the cooking spray and make pancakes with ¼ cup of batter per pancake. Add the strawberries to each pancake shortly after cooking begins. Do not pat the pancakes while cooking to maintain fluffy texture.
- Serve with syrup and enjoy!

Nutritional Information per serving Calories: 510 Fat: 27.8 g Carbohydrates: 59.3 g Protein: 11.9 g

Blueberry Walnut Pancakes

Servings: 4   **Serving size: Three pancakes**

Ingredients
- 2 cups buttermilk
- 1 large egg, beaten
- 1¾ cups flour
- 1½ tsps. baking powder
- 1 tsp. baking soda
- 1 tsp. sugar
- ½ tsp. salt
- 3 tbsps. unsalted butter
- ½ cup frozen blueberries
- ⅓ cup chopped walnuts

Directions Mix the buttermilk and eggs in a bowl.
In another bowl, mix the flour, baking powder, baking soda, sugar, and salt.
Add the buttermilk and eggs to the bowl with the dry ingredients and mix.
Allow the batter to sit for at least 15 minutes in the refrigerator, or overnight if possible.
Preheat a skillet to medium heat.
Wash the blueberries under cold water.
Spray the skillet with the cooking spray and make pancakes with ¼ cup of batter per pancake. Add the walnuts and blueberries to each pancake shortly after cooking begins. Do not pat the pancakes while cooking to maintain fluffy texture.
Serve with syrup and enjoy!

Nutritional Information per serving Calories: 422 Fat: 17.7 g Carbohydrates: 53.2 g Protein: 14 g

Carrot Cake Crepes

Servings: 6 crepes   **Serving size: One crepe**

Ingredients
- 1⅓ cups carrots
- ¾ cup low-fat milk
- 1 egg
- 1 tbsp. unsalted butter
- ½ tsp. vanilla extract
- ¾ cup whole wheat pastry flour

- 2 tbsps. sugar
- 2 tbsps. brown sugar
- 1 tsp. pumpkin pie spice
- ½ tsp. lemon zest
- ¼ tsp. table salt
- 2 cups chopped pineapple
- 3 tbsps. fat-free vanilla Greek yogurt

Directions Preheat a skillet pan to medium heat.
Chop the carrots into small pieces for blending.
Add the carrots, milk, egg, butter, and vanilla to a blender and blend until fully integrated.
Combine the flour, both sugars, pumpkin pie spice, lemon zest, and salt in a large bowl, pouring in the blended mix into the large bowl.
Spray the pan with cooking spray and add ¾ cup of batter per crepe, spreading evenly.
Cook the crepes for one to two minutes on each side.
Fill the crepes with Greek yogurt and pineapple pieces with enough to roll them up and enjoy!

Nutritional Information per serving Calories: 186 Fat: 3.3 g Carbohydrates: 34 g Protein: 6.1 g

Fruit Desserts

Fruit Parfait

Servings: 1 **Serving size: One bowl**

Ingredients
- 1 cup low fat plain Greek yogurt
- ¾ cup sliced strawberries or blueberries
- ¼ cup ancient grain granola

Directions
- Mix all the ingredients in a bowl and stir to fully incorporate. Enjoy!

Nutritional Information per serving Calories: 275 Fat: 4.1 g Carbohydrates: 45.7 g Protein: 15.3 g

Berries and Cream

Servings: 1 **Serving size: One bowl**

Ingredients
- 2 tbsps. mascarpone cheese
- 1 tbsp. heavy cream
- ¼ cup fresh strawberries, sliced
- 1 tbsp. fresh blueberries
- ½ tsp. pure vanilla extract
- 4 drops no sugar added liquid sweetener

Directions
- Mix the cheese in a hand mixer until spread out through the bowl.
- Mix in the vanilla, sweetener, and heavy cream to the bowl until soft.
- Transfer mixing contents to a large serving bowl, garnish with the strawberries around the cream, putting the blueberries on top.
- Serve and enjoy!

Nutritional Information per serving Calories: 183 Fat: 19 g Carbohydrates: 4 g Protein: 2 g

Blueberry Muffins

Servings: 12   **Serving size: One muffin**

Ingredients
- 1¾ cups plus 1 tsp. whole wheat flour
- 1 tsp. baking powder
- ½ tsp. baking soda
- ½ tsp. fine sea salt
- ⅓ cup olive oil
- ½ cup honey or maple syrup
- 2 eggs
- 1 cup plain Greek yogurt
- 2 tsps. vanilla extract
- 1 cup blueberries
- Cooking spray for muffin tray (ignore if using non-stick pan)

Directions Preheat the oven to 400º F.
Whisk together the flour with the baking powder, baking soda, salt, and cinnamon.
In another bowl, whisk together the oil and honey until consistent.
Add the eggs to the bowl with honey and whisk, mixing the yogurt and vanilla once the eggs are beaten.
Mix together both bowls and whisk to incorporate.
Add the blueberries and extra teaspoon flour to the bowl and fold into the batter.
Use the cooking spray on the muffin cups and fill with the batter three quarters of the way up. Sprinkle in the sugar to each muffin.
Bake for 16 to 19 minutes or until the muffins are golden brown.
Allow the muffins to cool before removing from the tray.
Serve and enjoy!

Nutritional Information per serving Calories: 197 Fat: 7.6 g Carbohydrates: 28.1/2 g Protein: 5.4 g

Banana Nut Muffins

Servings: 12   **Serving size: One muffin**

Ingredients
- 1 cup whole wheat flour
- ½ cup protein powder
- 1 tsp. baking powder
- ½ tsp. baking soda
- ¼ tsp. salt
- 2 tsps. ground cinnamon
- 1 tbsp. cornstarch
- 3 large extra ripe bananas
- 1 large egg
- 1 tbsp. oil
- 1 tsp. pure vanilla extract
- ¼ cup pancake or maple syrup or honey
- ¼ cup raw pecans or walnuts

Directions
- Preheat the oven to 425º F.
- Mash the ripe bananas.
- Mix the egg, bananas, oil, maple syrup, and vanilla in a bowl and whisk until the bananas are incorporated.
- In a separate bowl, mix the flour, protein powder, baking powder, baking soda, salt, cinnamon, and cornstarch. Whisk until all ingredients are well mixed.
- Mix the wet and dry bowls together, whisking to achieve a batter consistency.
- Fold the nuts in the batter until fully incorporated. Don't mix too hard, or else the batter consistency will be too hard.
- Spray the muffin tray, filling the cups with the batter until they reach ¾ capacity.
- Bake the muffins for five minutes at 425º, then lower the temperature to 375º and bake for 13 to 15 minutes more, until the muffins are golden brown.
- Let the muffins cool for five minutes, serve, and enjoy!

Nutritional Information per serving Calories: 108 Fat: 5 g Carbohydrates: 15 g Protein: 5 g

Strawberry and Raspberry Muffins

Servings: 12   **Serving size: One muffin**

Ingredients
- 3 cups all-purpose flour
- 1½ cups of sugar
- 4½ tsps. ground cinnamon
- 3 tsps. baking powder
- ½ tsp. salt
- ½ tsp. baking soda
- 2 eggs
- 1¼ cups whole milk
- 1 cup butter
- 1 cup fresh blueberries
- ½ cup fresh raspberries
- ½ cup chopped fresh strawberries
- Cooking spray for the muffin tray.

Directions Preheat the oven to 375º F. and a skillet to medium heat.
Wash all the berries under cold water.
In one bowl, mix the flour, sugar, cinnamon, baking powder, salt, and baking soda. Whisk until mixed well.
Melt the butter in the skillet and transfer to another bowl.
In the bowl with the butter, mix the milk, the butter, and the eggs and whisk until the ingredients are fully incorporated.
Mix together contents of both bowls and beat the batter until fully formed, folding in the berries.
Spray the muffin tray with cooking spray and bake for 18-20 minutes, or until muffins are golden brown.
Let cool for five minutes, serve, and enjoy!

Nutritional Information per serving Calories: 359 Fat: 17.2 g Carbohydrates: 45.1/2 g Protein: 5.2 g

Berries and Cream Tart

Servings: 8   **Serving size: ⅛ of total tart.**

Ingredients

For the crust:
- ½ cup unsalted butter,
- ⅔ cup granulated sugar
- ½ tsp. vanilla extract
- ¼ tsp. almond extract
- 1 large egg
- 1 cup plus 2 tbsps. all-purpose flour
- ¼ tsp. baking powder
- ¼ tsp. salt

For the frosting:
- 4 oz. cream cheese
- ⅔ cup powdered sugar
- ¼ tsp. vanilla extract
- 2 drops of almond extract
- 1 cup chilled heavy whipping cream

Directions Preheat the oven to 350º F.
Use a hand mixer to mix the butter and sugar, adding in the eggs and vanilla extract and beating until fully incorporated.
Add the flour and baking soda, adding water as needed if the dough gets too hard.
Get a 9½ in. tart pan and pour the batter into it over parchment paper.
Wet your fingers with water and use them to press the dough into the sides, making sure each side is covered evenly.
Bake for 12-15 minutes until the edges just begin to turn golden brown.
Once the baking is done and the tart crust has cooled, transfer the baked product to the refrigerator for at least 30 minutes.
While it cools, clean the hand mixer and bowl.
Microwave the cream cheese for ten seconds to soften.
Mix the cream cheese, powdered sugar, vanilla, and almond extract in the mixer, until completely integrated and soft.
Remove the crust using a butter knife, being careful not to crack the tart, removing the parchment paper.
Spread the cream on the crust and assort the berries on top.
Cut into eight slices, serve, and enjoy!

Nutritional Information per serving Calories: 424 Fat: 28 g Carbohydrates: 40 g Protein: 4 g

Wonton Cherry Pie

Servings: 1   **Serving size: One pie**

Ingredients
- 1 square pre-packed wonton
- 1 tbsp. premade light cherry pie filling
- 1 egg
- 1 dash cinnamon sugar

Directions Preheat the oven to 375º F.
Add a tablespoon of filling to the wonton.
Separate the yolk from the egg and brush the pie with it.
Bake for seven to ten minutes on a baking tray with parchment paper.
Let the pie sit for three minutes until cool.
Serve and enjoy!

Nutritional Information per serving Calories: 60 Fat: 0.3 g Carbohydrates: 11/2 g Protein: 3.4 g

Wonton Raspberry Pie

Servings: 1   **Serving size: One pie**

Ingredients
- 1 square pre-packed wonton
- 1 tbsp. premade raspberry pie filling
- 1 egg
- 1 dash cinnamon sugar

Directions
1. Preheat the oven to 375º F.
2. Add a tablespoon of filling to the wonton.
3. Separate the yolk from the egg and brush the pie with it.
4. Bake for seven to ten minutes on a baking tray with parchment paper.
5. Let the pie sit for three minutes until cool.
6. Serve and enjoy!

Nutritional Information per serving Calories: 93 Fat: 2.4 g Carbohydrates: 13 g Protein: 4.3 g

Wonton Apple Pie

Servings: 1   **Serving size: One pie**

Ingredients
- 1 square pre-packed wonton
- 1 tbsp. premade apple pie filling
- 1 egg
- 1 dash cinnamon sugar

Directions Preheat the oven to 375º F.
Add a tablespoon of filling to the wonton.
Separate the yolk from the egg and brush the pie with it.
Bake for seven to ten minutes on a baking tray with parchment paper.
Let the pie sit for three minutes until cool.
Serve and enjoy!

Nutritional Information per serving Calories: 95 Fat: 2.4 g Carbohydrates: 13.1/2 g Protein: 4.3 g

Wonton Blueberry Pie

Servings: 1 **Serving size: One pie**

Ingredients
- 1 square pre-packed wonton
- 1 tbsp. premade blueberry pie filling
- 1 egg
- 1 dash cinnamon sugar

Directions Preheat the oven to 375º F.
Add a tablespoon of filling to the wonton.
Separate the yolk from the egg and brush the pie with it.
Bake for seven to ten minutes on a baking tray with parchment paper.
Let the pie sit for three minutes until cool.
Serve and enjoy!

Nutritional Information per serving Calories: 100 Fat: 2.4 g Carbohydrates: 14.8 g Protein: 4.4 g

Macro Oatmeal Raisin Cookies

Servings: 12 **Serving size: One cookie**

Ingredients
- 1⅓ cups oats rolled oats or quick cooking
- ¾ cup all purpose flour
- A pinch of salt
- ¼ tsp. baking powder
- ¼ tsp. baking soda
- 1 tsp. cinnamon ground
- 1 tsp. vanilla
- 6 tbsps. unsalted butter
- ¾ cup light brown sugar
- 1 egg
- ¾ cup raisins
- ¾ cup flax seeds

Directions Preheat the oven to 350º F.
Line a baking tray with parchment paper.
Mix the butter and brown sugar in a mixer bowl for one to two minutes.
Add the egg, cinnamon, and vanilla and mix until all ingredients are mixed properly.
In another bowl, mix the flax seeds, oats, raisins, salt, and baking soda.
Mix together the contents of both bowls, folding to fully incorporate.
Make tablespoon sized-balls and lay them over the parchment paper, separating them by ½ inch from one another.
Bake the cookies for 12 minutes for a chewy cookie, or 14 minutes for a crunchy cookie.
Let the cookies rest for five minutes before serving. Enjoy!

Nutritional Information per serving Calories: 207 Fat: 8 g Carbohydrates: 30 g Protein: 3 g

Macro Strawberry Macadamia Nut Cookies

Servings: 10 **Serving size: One cookie**

Ingredients
- 1 cup almond flour
- ½ cup erythritol or other sugar substitute
- ¼ cup butter, unsalted
- 1 tsp. vanilla extract
- ½ tsp. almond extract
- ½ cup macadamia nuts
- ½ cup fresh strawberries

Directions Preheat the oven to 350º F.
Preheat a skillet to medium heat.
Wash and chop the strawberries into four pieces, removing the stems.
Melt the butter in the skillet.
In a large bowl, mix together the melted butter, erythritol, vanilla, and almond until smooth and add the almond flour.

Fold the macadamia nuts and strawberries into the batter, being careful not to mash the strawberries or the nuts.
Separate the dough into ten equal balls and separate them on a baking tray lined with parchment paper.
Bake for 10-12 minutes.
Let rest for five minutes, serve and enjoy!

Nutritional Information per serving Calories: 162 Fat: 15 g Carbohydrates: 4 g Protein: 3 g

Dairy Desserts

Macro Banana Protein Smoothie

Servings: 4   Serving size: One fourth of total smoothie

Ingredients
- ¾ cup nonfat Greek yogurt
- 2 cups of bananas
- 1 tsp. vanilla extract
- ¼ cup vanilla protein powder
- 2 cups skim milk, or any other milk of your choice

Directions Cut the bananas into slices.
Spread the yogurt over an ice cube tray.
Freeze the yogurt and bananas overnight.
Place all ingredients in a blender and puree until smooth.
Serve and enjoy!

Nutritional Information per serving Calories: 294 Fat: 3.1 g Carbohydrates: 34.3 g Protein: 33.7 g

Macro Berry Smoothie

Servings: 1

Ingredients
- ¾ cup strawberries
- ¾ cup raspberries
- ¾ cup blueberries
- ¼ cup bananas
- ½ cup skim milk
- ½ scoop protein powder

Directions Cut the bananas into small slices.
Cut and halve the strawberries, removing the green stems.
Put all the ingredients in the blender and puree until smooth.

Nutritional Information per serving Calories: 202 Fat: 1.6 g Carbohydrates: 31.9 g Protein: 16.7 g

Macro Pumpkin Pie

Servings: 8   Serving size: ⅛ slice of the pie.

Ingredients
- 16 oz. Greek yogurt cream cheese
- 10 oz. plain or vanilla nonfat Greek yogurt
- 3 large eggs
- ½ cup 2% milk
- 3 scoops protein powder
- 1 tsp. vanilla extract
- A dash of salt
- 15 oz. canned 100% pumpkin
- Cooking spray for the pan

Directions Allow the cream cheese, eggs, and yogurt to sit out until they reach room temperature.
Preheat the oven to 300º F.
Microwave the cream cheese for ten sounds and mash to soften.
Add the cream cheese yogurt to the hand mixer and blend until mixed.
Add the protein powder and mix for another three minutes.
Spray the cooking pan. and add the mixture.
Bake for 25 to 30 minutes and then lower the heat to 180º and bake for another 30 to 35 minutes, allowing the oven to be slightly open.
Let it cool outside the oven for 20 minutes and then transfer to the refrigerator, allowing it to chill overnight.
Serve and enjoy!

Nutritional Information per serving Calories: 407 Fat: 22.1/2 g Carbohydrates: 13.6 g Protein: 38.4 g

Macro Sweet Potato Pie

Servings: 10   **Serving size: 1/10 slice of the pie.**

Ingredients

For the crust:
- 1 cup whole wheat flour
- ½ tsp. salt
- 4 tbsps. unsalted butter,
- 2 tsps. nonfat milk
- 1 tsp. pure maple syrup
- ¾ tsp vanilla extract
- 1-2 tbsps. ice cold water
- Cooking spray for baking

For the filling:
- 1¾ cups cooked and mashed sweet potato or yams
- ¼ cup plain nonfat Greek yogurt
- 6 tbsps. confectioners' style erythritol
- 1 tsp. ground cinnamon
- ¼ tsp. ground allspice
- ¼ tsp. ground nutmeg
- ¼ tsp. ground cloves
- ¼ tsp. ground ginger
- ¼ tsp. salt
- ½ cup nonfat milk
- 2 tsps. vanilla extract
- 1¼ tsps. liquid sweetener
- 3 large egg whites

Directions

Crust: Mix the flour and the salt in a bowl.
Add the butter by cutting it in and mix.
Whisk together the milk, maple syrup, vanilla, and two tsps. of water in another bowl. Drizzle it over the flour mixture and mix.
Add water one teaspoon at a time until it reaches a dough consistency.
Transfer the dough to plastic wrap and fold it over, making a pie crust shape.
Chill the dough for 30 minutes.
Preheat the oven to 375º F.

Filling: Mix the sweet potato in a blender with the yogurt.
Sprinkle the erythritol, cinnamon, allspice, nutmeg, cloves, ginger, and salt as it blends.
Pour in the milk, vanilla extract, and liquid sweetener until fully mixed.
Add the egg whites and blend until fully mixed.
Place the dough in a pie tray for baking, spraying with cooking spray.
Press the dough into the tray.
Bake the dough for 25 minutes.
Remove from the oven and add the filling, baking for another 25-30 minutes at 350º.
Cool the pie to room temperature.
Put the pie in the refrigerator for eight hours before serving.
Slice pieces of the pie and enjoy!

Nutritional Information per serving Calories: 127 Fat: 4.1/2 g Carbohydrates: 18.4 g Protein: 4.1 g

Macro Carrot Cake

Servings: 6 **Serving size: 1/6 slice of the cake.**

Ingredients
- 2 medium carrots
- ⅓ cups pitted dates
- ⅓ cups whole grain flour
- ¼ cup vanilla whey protein powder (Change it to soy protein powder for vegan variation)
- 3 egg whites
- ½ tsp. baking powder
- ¼ tsp. each of ground cinnamon, nutmeg, ginger, and cloves
- ¼ tsp. salt
- Cooking spray for baking

Directions
- Preheat the oven to 350º F.
- Grate the carrots to a pulp-like shape.
- Chop the dates and remove the seeds. The dates should look like a paste afterward.
- Mix the dates and the carrots in a blender until fully integrated.
- Mix all ingredients together in a hand mixer until a batter consistency is reached.
- Line a baking tray with aluminum foil and spray with the cooking spray.
- Pour the batter on the tray.
- Bake for forty minutes.
- Let the cake cool to room temperature before serving.
- Serve and enjoy!

Nutritional Information per serving Calories: 114 Fat: 0.8 g Carbohydrates: 18.1/2 g Protein: 9½ g

Macro Key Lime Pie

Servings: 10 **Serving size: 1/10 slice of the pie.**

Ingredients

For the Crust:
- 2½ cups Graham crackers
- ¼ tsp. salt
- ⅔ cup unsweetened vanilla almond milk
- 1 tsp. natural butter flavoring.

For the filling:
- 12 oz. evaporated fat free milk
- 1 tsp. liquid stevia extract
- 120g (1 cup) dried nonfat milk
- ½ tbsp. powdered erythritol or other sweetener
- ½ tsp. xanthan gum
- 4 large egg yolks
- 10 g organic corn starch
- ¼ plain, nonfat Greek yogurt
- 1 tsp. key lime zest
- ¾ cup key lime juice

Directions Preheat the oven to 350º F. The crust will be made first.
Crumble the graham crackers and mix with all the other ingredients for the crust and press into a 9½ in. bowl for baking.
Bake for 13 minutes, until firm. As it's baking, prepare to make the filling.
Blend the evaporated milk and sweetener in a hand mixer.
Whisk in the milk powder, sweetener, and xanthan gum.
Add in the egg yolks, corn starch, yogurt, and lime zest.
Mix in the blender until completely smooth, with a pudding-like texture.
Pour the filling onto the crust and return to the oven, baking for another 16 minutes.
Let it cool for two hours before refrigerating overnight.
Cut into ten pieces, serve, and enjoy!

Nutritional Information per serving Calories: 250 Fat: 7 g Carbohydrates: 37 g Protein: 10 g

Macro Chocolate Chip Cookies

Servings: 24   **Serving size: One cookie**

Ingredients
- 1 cup butter
- ½ cup no sugar sweetener
- 2 eggs
- 2 tsps. molasses
- 1 cup vanilla protein powder
- ½ tsp. salt
- 2 tsps. baking soda
- 2½ cups whole wheat flour
- 1 cup dark chocolate chips

Directions Preheat the oven to 375° F.
Mix the butter and the sweetener in a bowl until fluffy.
Add in the eggs and molasses, beating until properly mixed.
Add vanilla protein powder, salt, baking soda, and flour and beat until mixed.
Add the dark chocolate chips, folding to mix in with the batter.
Roll the dough into 24 identical balls. Spread over the sheet at least half an inch apart, pressing down each ball gently.
Bake for eight to nine minutes, or until just golden brown.
Serve and enjoy!

Nutritional Information per serving Calories: 175 Fat: 11 g Carbohydrates: 15 g Protein: 6 g

Mitarashi Dango (Japanese Sweet Dumplings)

Servings: 8 skewers   **Serving size: One skewer with four dumplings**

Ingredients

For the dumplings:
- 1 ½ cups glutinous rice flour
- 1 tsp sugar
- 180ml water

For the sauce:
- 1 cup of water
- 2 tbsps. sugar
- 1½ tbsps. soy sauce
- 2 tsps. potato starch

Directions

Dumplings: Preheat a saucepan filled with water and bring to a boil.
Mix the rice flour and sugar in a bowl.
Slowly mix in the water and knead—the desired consistency should feel like an earlobe.
Roll into small balls one inch in diameter and boil until they're floating. Boil for two minutes.
Remove the dumplings from the boiling water to another bowl with cold water to cool down.
Once cooled, skewer the dumplings with the bamboo sticks or serve on a small plate.

Sauce: Mix all the ingredients gently in a whisking bowl.
Drizzle over the dumplings and enjoy!

Nutritional Information per serving Calories: 197 Fat: 0 g Carbohydrates: 45.8 g Protein: 2.7 g

Macro Cheesecake

Ingredients

For the Crust:
- ½ cups vanilla wafers
- 4 tbsps. light butter
- Cooking spray for the pan.

For the Cheesecake:
- 8 oz. fat free cream cheese
- 8 oz. fat free cottage cheese
- 2 whole eggs
- ⅓ cups Protein powder
- 3 tbsp. sugar free cheesecake pudding mix
- 3 tbsps. no sugar added sweetener
- 1/4 cups white chocolate

Directions Preheat the oven to 310º F.
Line a baking dish with aluminum foil and spray with cooking spray.
Crumble the cookies and mix with the butter in a hand mixer.
Spray the tray with the cooking spray.
Press the crust onto the foil and bake for ten minutes.
Mix all filling ingredients in a clean blender bowl until mixed to a fluffy consistency.
Pour the filling into the crust and bake for another 50 minutes.
In a double boiler, melt the white chocolate during the last few minutes of cooking.
Let it cool at room temperature after baking and pour the white chocolate on top.
Refrigerate for five to six hours.
Serve and enjoy!

Nutritional Information Calories: 286 Fat: 21.3 g Carbohydrates: 17.5 g Protein: 11.2 g

Macro Tiramisu

Servings: 10   **Serving size: One tenth of total cake**

Ingredients

For the cake:
- ¾ cup no sugar added sweetener
- ¾ cup butter
- 3 large eggs
- ¼ cup heavy cream
- 1 tsp. vanilla extract
- 1½ cups Wholesome Yum Blanched almond flour
- 1 tsp. baking powder
- ⅛ tsp. sea salt

For the drizzle:
- ¼ cup espresso or other strong coffee

For the filling:
- 4 large egg yolks
- 3 tbsps. no sugar added sweetener
- 1 cup mascarpone cheese
- 1 cup heavy cream
- ½ tsp. cocoa powder for dusting

Directions Preheat the oven to 350º F.
Line a 9-in. square pan with parchment paper.
In a large bowl, beat the sweetener and butter until soft peaks form.
Add the eggs, heavy cream, and vanilla extract and beat until it softens.
Add the almond flour, baking powder, and salt, beating until smooth.
Transfer the dough to the tray and bake for 20-25 minutes.
Prepare a double boiler on the stove and bring the water to a boil.
Separate the egg yolks and mix with sweetener in the double boiler. Lower to a simmer and cook for another seven to ten minutes.
Mix the eggs in a mixer until they're lemony yellow.
Whip the heavy cream in a separate bowl until smooth peaks form.
Mix the mascarpone with the yolks and beat until smooth.
Mix the two bowls, folding in the mascarpone.
Take the cake off the tray and place onto a cutting board.
Pour the espresso over the cake.
Cut the cake in half and put the filling on top of one half, and top with the rest of the filling.
Sift the cocoa powder over the cake.
Refrigerate for at least four hours. Serve and enjoy!

Nutritional Information per serving Calories: 270 Fat: 25.7 g Carbohydrates: 7.4 g Protein: 7.4 g

Macro Rice Pudding

Servings: 4   **Serving size: 01/4 of total recipe**

Ingredients
- 2¼ cups unsweetened almond milk
- 1¼ cups water
- 1 cup white rice
- 1 tsp. ground cinnamon
- ¾ cup coconut milk
- ¼ cup no sugar added sweetener
- 2 scoops vanilla protein powder

Directions
- Preheat a medium pot to medium heat on the stove.
- Add the almond milk, water, rice, vanilla, and cinnamon to the pot. Simmer for 20 minutes.
- Stir in the protein powder, sweetener, coconut milk, and stir.
- Serve and enjoy.

Nutritional Information per serving Calories: 289 Fat: 7.3 g Carbohydrates: 40.7 g Protein: 15.8 g

Macro Ice Cream Sundae

Servings: 1

Ingredients
- 3 small scoops of Birthday Cake Ice Cream (117 g)
- 17 g peanut butter protein bar

Directions
- Cut the protein bar into small pieces and crumble over the ice cream.
- Serve and enjoy!

Nutritional Information per serving Calories: 201 Fat: 8.4 g Carbohydrates: 29 g Protein: 15.4 g

Chapter 13: Two-Week Programs

Let's See This in Action!

Now that you've seen some of the recipes this book offers, let's talk more about the two-week programs you can try out if you're curious to know how this diet can work for you. You can calculate your intake of calories and other nutrients throughout the day. This book will give you a template of how you can plan your own meals. Use the recipes and what you have learned in this book to help plan your two-week meals. It's impossible to know your macro needs without consulting your doctor and knowing your BMR and exercise regimen. Still, you should now have a good idea of what to expect when pursuing the Macro diet.

You may also have to substitute meals within their programs to account for a vegetarian or vegan diet if the meals have animal products. Anyone can follow along with the Macro diet and improve their health regardless of their dietary restrictions.

The first two-week diet plan is based on men aged 35/40 years, with an average body weight of 80 kg, and average height of 180 cm. Sedentary.

BMR is 1790. Recommended total daily calories for weight loss are 1843.

Two-Week Program for Men

WEEK ONE:

Sunday

Breakfast: Egg and Chicken Breakfast Bites

Snack: Roast Beef and Cheddar Cheese Rolls

Lunch: Chicken and Lentil Soup

Dinner: Beef Burrito

Dessert: Wonton Blueberry Pie

Calorie total: 1427

Protein total: 80

Carbohydrate total: 131.3

Fat Total: 58.8

Monday

Breakfast: Pumpkin Spice Waffles

Snack: Cucumber Turkey Sliders

Lunch: White Bean and Kale Soup

Dinner: Eggplant and Rice Stew

Dessert: Berries and Cream Tart

Calorie total: 1400

Protein total: 118.4
Carbohydrate total: 155.6

Fat Total: 64.8

Tuesday

Breakfast: Breakfast Oatmeal Cookies
Snack: Garlic Garbanzo Beans
Lunch: Pork Ramen with Zucchini Noodles
Dinner: Root Vegetable and Pork Stew
Dessert: Banana Nut Muffins

Calorie total: 1828
Protein total: 100.3
Carbohydrate total: 153.8
Fat Total: 89.9

Wednesday

Breakfast: Egg Salad Sub
Snack: Whole Wheat Roast Beef Crackers
Lunch: Macro Chowder
Dinner: Juicy Skillet Pork Chops
Dessert: Macro Carrot Cake

Calorie total: 1480
Protein total: 134.3
Carbohydrate total: 175.4
Fat Total: 54.9

Thursday

Breakfast: Breakfast sandwich
Snack: Mango Wrapped in Turkey
Lunch: Chilled Cucumber Soup
Dinner: Japanese Chicken Curry
Dessert: Macro Oatmeal Raisin Cookies

Calorie total: 1563
Protein total: 133.6
Carbohydrate total: 146
Fat Total: 47.6

Friday

Breakfast: Blueberry Walnut Pancakes
Snack: Ham and Cheese Rolls
Lunch: Tofu Ginger Salad
Dinner: Baked Lemon Salmon with Wild Rice
Dessert: Macro Berry Smoothie

Calorie total: 1544
Protein total: 124.6
Carbohydrate total: 143.2
Fat Total: 55.3

Saturday

Breakfast: Whole Wheat Crepes with Kiwis

Snack: Salami and Provolone Cheese Rolls

Lunch: Potato Zucchini Vichyssoise

Dinner: Chicken and Black Bean Stew

Dessert: Macro Tiramisu

Calorie total: 1535

Protein total: 85.9

Carbohydrate total: 157.6

Fat Total: 66.2

WEEK TWO:

Sunday

Breakfast: Whole Wheat Waffles and Cream

Snack: Dried Apples with Nuts

Lunch: Fish and Vegetable Soup

Dinner: Gazpacho with Scallop Skewers

Dessert: Macro Berry Smoothie

Calorie total: 1524

Protein total: 84.4

Carbohydrate total: 150.9

Fat Total: 67.8

Monday

Breakfast: Macro Italian Sub

Snack: Whole Wheat Ham Crackers

Lunch: Powerful Chicken Noodle Soup

Dinner: Seasonal Pumpkin Salad

Dessert: Macro Pumpkin Pie

Calorie total: 1695

Protein total: 112.6

Carbohydrate total: 124

Fat Total: 172.4

Tuesday

Breakfast: Fruit Parfait

Snack: Whole Wheat Crackers and Artichoke Dip

Lunch: Chilled Asparagus Bisque

Dinner: Artichoke Heart Salad

Dessert: Macro Banana Protein Smoothie

Calorie total: 1508

Protein total: 82.6

Carbohydrate total: 162.5

Fat Total: 105.6

Wednesday

Breakfast: Triple Berry Oatmeal

Snack: Chocolate and Coconut Protein Balls

Lunch: Chicken Goulash
Dinner: One Pot Pork Stew
Dessert: Macro Ice Cream Sundae
Calorie total: 1555

Protein total: 75.3
Carbohydrate total: 141.3
Fat Total: 92.6

Thursday

Breakfast: Macro Egg Sandwich
Snack: Whole Wheat Tuna Crackers
Lunch: Powerful Chicken Noodle Soup
Dinner: Beef Gyro
Dessert: Macro Rice Pudding

Calorie total: 1844
Protein total: 83,6
Carbohydrate total: 148,4
Fat Total: 61,3

Friday

Breakfast: Pumpkin Crepes with Pumpkin Filling
Snack: Sliced Carrots and Hummus
Lunch: Lamb Gyro
Dinner: Stuffed Pepper Soup

Dessert: Wonton Cherry Pie
Calorie total: 1856
Protein total: 139,9
Carbohydrate total: 132,8
Fat Total: 67,7

Saturday

Breakfast: Breakfast Wrap
Snack: Chocolate Oat Bars
Lunch: Chicken Posole
Dinner: Hamburger Salad
Dessert: Wonton Raspberry Pie

Calorie total: 1586
Protein total: 118,6
Carbohydrate total: 119,2
Fat Total: 71

This two-week diet plan is based on women aged 35/40 years, average body weight of 70 kg, and average height of 170 cm. Sedentary.

BMR is 1445. Recommended total daily calories for weight loss are 1488.

Two-Week Program for Women

WEEK ONE:

Sunday

Breakfast: Carrot Cake Crepes
Snack: Hard-Boiled Eggs with Apples and Carrots
Lunch: Pork Tenderloin Sandwich
Dinner: Leftover Thanksgiving Turkey Stew
Dessert: Frozen Coconut Sorbet
Calorie total: 1331
Protein total: 80,6
Carbohydrate total: 135,9
Fat Total: 46,6

Monday

Breakfast: Macro Key Lime Pie
Snack: Open-Faced Spinach and Cheese Melt
Lunch: Garlic Grilled Shrimp
Dinner: Macro Garden Salad (with Macro Italian Dressing)
Dessert: Macro Rice Pudding
Calorie total: 1435,6
Protein total: 85,8
Carbohydrate total: 132,8
Fat Total: 58,3

Tuesday

Breakfast: Peanut Batter and Banana Pancakes
Snack: Vegan Bean Burrito
Lunch: Macro Chicken Pot Pie
Dinner: Stuffed Pepper Soup
Dessert: Macro Chocolate Chip Cookies
Calorie total: 1519
Protein total: 88
Carbohydrate total: 124
Fat Total: 48

Wednesday

Breakfast: Cucunber with Mango Salsa
Snack: Peanut Butter and Strawberry Celery Sticks

Lunch: Tochitura de Pui
Dinner: Turkey Burgers
Dessert: Whole Wheat Pancakes and Berries
Calorie total: 1345

Protein total: 91
Carbohydrate total: 79,9
Fat Total: 34,9

Thursday

Breakfast: Blueberry Muffins
Snack: Sliced Apple and Peanut Butter
Lunch: Macro Roast Beef
Dinner: Pea and Mint Soup
Dessert: Macro Strawberry and Macadamia Nut Cookies

Calorie total: 1431
Protein total: 95,6
Carbohydrate total: 122,5
Fat Total: 55

Friday

Breakfast: Macro Banana Protein Smoothie
Snack: Macro Avocado Toast
Lunch: Roast Beef Po' Boy
Dinner: Hearty Vegetable Stew
Dessert: Classic Ambrosia

Calorie total: 1177
Protein total: 84,7
Carbohydrate total: 110,3
Fat Total: 45,1

Saturday

Breakfast: Dried Apples with Nuts
Snack: Hard-Boiled Eggs with Apples and Carrots
Lunch: Cold Beet Soup
Dinner: Grilled Turkey Breast

Dessert: Mitarashi Dango
Calorie total: 1317,4
Protein total: 62,5
Carbohydrate total: 118,7
Fat Total: 61,2

WEEK TWO:

Sunday

Breakfast: Mango Wrapped in Turkey
Snack: Sliced Pears and Almond Butter
Lunch: Buffalo Chicken Stew
Dinner: Macro Cobb Salad (with Dijon Vinagrette)

Dessert: Frozen Pineapple and Yogurt Rings
Calorie total: 1478
Protein total: 136,9
Carbohydrate total: 105
Fat Total: 65,7

Monday

Breakfast: Triple Berry Oatmeal
Snack: Roast Beef and Cheddar Cheese Rolls
Lunch: Stuffed Pepper Soup
Dinner: Cooked Eggplant Salad
Dessert: Peanut Butter and Banana Pancakes

Calorie total: 1361
Protein total: 63
Carbohydrate total: 116,2
Fat Total: 67,5

Tuesday

Breakfast: Salami and Provolone Cheese Rolls
Snack: Vegan Chickpea Gyro
Lunch: Juicy Skillet Pork Chops
Dinner: Grilled Pork with Soy Sauce Marinade
Dessert: Macro Key Lime Pie

Calorie total: 1259
Protein total: 91,8
Carbohydrate total: 97,5
Fat Total: 69,7

Wednesday

Breakfast: Cucumber Ham Sliders
Snack: Whole Wheat Tuna Crackers
Lunch: Tuna Salad Sub
Dinner: Gazpacho with Scallop Skewers
Dessert: Macro Tiramisu

Calorie total: 1323
Protein total: 104,1
Carbohydrate total: 68,2
Fat Total: 58,5

Thursday

Breakfast: Macro Carrot Cake
Snack: Whole Wheat Crackers and Artichoke Dip
Lunch: Chicken Noodle Stew
Dinner: Turkey Shish Kebabs
Dessert: Berries and Cream Tart
Calorie total: 1346
Protein total: 86,7
Carbohydrate total: 110,9
Fat Total: 63,2

Friday

Breakfast: Chocolate Oat Bars
Snack: Sliced Carrots and Hummus
Lunch: Skinless Chicken Ramen
Dinner: Roast Turkey Salad
Dessert: Frozen Yogurt Pretzels
Calorie total: 1454
Protein total: 107,7
Carbohydrate total: 132,6
Fat Total: 61

Saturday

Breakfast: Egg and Chicken Breakfast Bites
Snack: Garlic Garbanzo Beans
Lunch: Macro Egg Sandwich
Dinner: Spinach and Arugula Salad
Dessert: Macro Pumpkin Pie
Calorie total: 1449
Protein total: 105
Carbohydrate total: 108,6
Fat Total: 68,3

Conclusion

Now that you've seen the programs and you know what a sample of it might look like for you, nothing is stopping you from seeking the best possible changes in yourself. The Macro diet is here to help you find the way to live your best life with delicious recipes. Perhaps this cookbook has inspired you to help others pursue this diet for their own health or has improved your self-esteem. There is nowhere to go from here but up.

Finally, a word for those who are feeling mounting pressure to succeed. It's okay if you fail when pursuing this diet. You're a human being, and you will fail in many aspects of your life. What's important is that you learn from it, forgive yourself, and keep going. Remember, the only actual failure is quitting, and so long as you don't do that, you'll succeed in this diet.

Thank you for reading this far, and whatever your goals may be, just know that so long as you believe in yourself, there is nothing you can't do.

References

BMR Calculator. (2019). Calculator.net. https://www.calculator.net/bmr-calculator.html

Carbohydrates and the Glycemic Index: "Slow" Carbs vs. "Fast" Carbs. (n.d.). Retrieved July 6, 2021, from https://www.kumc.edu/Documents/cray/Glycemic%20Index.pdf

February 5, A. B., & 2020. (2020, February 5). *10 Healthy Salad Dressing Brands to Buy in 2020 (and 11 to Avoid).* Eat This Not That. https://www.eatthis.com/healthy-salad-dressing/

Fryar, C. (2018). The Narrative of Ann Pratt: Life-Writing, Genre and Bureaucracy in a Postemancipation Scandal. *History Workshop Journal, 85*(122), 265–279. https://doi.org/10.1093/hwj/dby001

Harvard School of Public Health. (2018, July 24). *Types of Fat.* The Nutrition Source. https://www.hsph.harvard.edu/nutritionsource/what-should-you-eat/fats-and-cholesterol/types-of-fat/

HISTORY OF MACROBIOTICS | The Macrobiotic Association. (n.d.). The Macrobiotic Association. Retrieved July 4, 2021, from https://macrobiotics.org.uk/history-of-macrobiotics/

Hwu, A. (2005). *Physical Activity and Controlling Weight.* https://www.k-state.edu/paccats/Contents/PA/PDF/Physical%20Activity%20and%20Controlling%20Weight.pdf

Julson, E. (2018, June 5). *IIFYM (If It Fits Your Macros): A Beginner's Guide.* Healthline; Healthline Media. https://www.healthline.com/nutrition/iifym-guide

Nutrition Basics | at WSU. (2019). Wsu.edu. https://mynutrition.wsu.edu/nutrition-basics

Ronald Ernst Kotzsch. (1986). *Macrobiotics : yesterday and today.* Japan Publications.

Shanti Menon. (2018, January 9). *Mercury Guide.* NRDC. https://www.nrdc.org/stories/mercury-guide

Slow-release carbs list. (2019, June 27). Www.medicalnewstoday.com. https://www.medicalnewstoday.com/articles/325586

The Ultimate Guide to Pre and Post-Workout Carbohydrates. (2015, July 6). Life by Daily Burn. https://dailyburn.com/life/health/carbohydrates-pre-post-workout-carbs/

Cozza, S. (n.d.). *Cuban From Miami Recipe by Tasty.* Tasty.co. Retrieved September 21, 2021, from https://tasty.co/recipe/cuban-from-miami

Hegner, K. (2015, May 5). *Turkey, Havarti Spinach Panini.* Chocolate Slopes®. https://www.chocolateslopes.com/havarti-turkey-and-spinach-panini/

Low Calorie Meatball Sandwich Recipe - 5 Points | LaaLoosh. (2010, April 15). Laa Loosh. https://www.laaloosh.com/2010/04/15/low-calorie-meatball-sandwich-recipe/

Pretty Pink Bullets. (n.d.). *Classic Cuban Midnight (Medianoche) Sandwich.* Allrecipes. Retrieved September 21, 2021, from https://www.allrecipes.com/recipe/43945/classic-cuban-midnight-medianoche-sandwich/#nutrition

Sam. (2017, May 21). *Skinny Shrimp Po Boy.* The Culinary Compass. https://www.theculinarycompass.com/skinny-shrimp-po-boy/

Teaspoon, T. (2020, January 31). *Hot and Toasty Open Faced Spinach Melts.* Tara Teaspoon. https://taratsp..com/spinach-melts/

Acheson, H. (2019, November). *Leftover Turkey Gumbo.* EatingWell. https://www.eatingwell.com/recipe/276372/leftover-turkey-gumbo/

Buffalo Chicken Stew. (2018, September 28). So Delicious. https://sodelicious.recipes/recipe/buffalo-chicken-stew/

Eb. (2018, October 16). *Easy Chicken Goulash.* Easy Peasy Foodie. https://www.easypeasyfoodie.com/easy-chicken-goulash/

Frost, A. (n.d.). *Frosty Web.* Frosty Web. Retrieved September 22, 2021, from https://cyberfrosty.com/recipes?recipe=Japanese%20Turkey%20Curry

Hanlon, J. (2009, January 14). *Cajun Chicken and Sausage Gumbo.* Allrecipes. https://www.allrecipes.com/recipe/141114/cajun-chicken-and-sausage-gumbo/

Jenn. (2020, December 8). *Easy, Chicken and Black Bean Soup.* A Dash of Macros. https://adashofmacros.com/chicken-black-bean-soup/

Low-Calorie Katsu Chicken Curry. (n.d.). Lo-Dough. Retrieved September 22, 2021, from https://lodough.co/blogs/recipes/katsu-chicken-curry

Perry, S. (2018, February 14). *My Mom's Venezuelan Chupe*. Allrecipes. https://www.allrecipes.com/recipe/262058/my-moms-venezuelan-chupe/

says, L. (2015, January 7). *Light Creamy Chicken Noodle Soup*. Sally's Baking Addiction. https://sallysbakingaddiction.com/lightened-creamy-chicken-noodle-soup/

Slusher, A. (2017, November 3). *Leftover Turkey (or Chicken) Soup Recipe*. Simply so Healthy. https://simplysohealthy.com/leftover-turkey-chicken-soup/

Whereismyspoon. (2017, June 20). *Romanian Sausage Stew - Tochitura*. Where Is My Spoon. https://whereismyspoon.co/moldavian-stew-with-cheese-and-eggs/

Baier, L. (2021, March 1). *Healthy Oven Roasted Chicken*. A Sweet Pea Chef. https://www.asweetpeachef.com/healthy-oven-roasted-chicken/

Chicken Katsudon. (2020, June 14). Norecipes - Elevating Everyday Meals. https://norecipes.com/chicken-katsudon/

Clarke, E. (2020, April 23). *Healthy Chicken Pot Pie*. Well Plated by Erin. https://www.wellplated.com/healthy-chicken-pot-pie/

Delicious, C. @ D. (2014, May 23). *Lighter General Tso's Chicken - Damn Delicious*. Damn Delicious. https://damndelicious.net/2014/05/23/lighter-general-tsos-chicken/

Gore, M. (2019, April 29). *This Turkey Burger Is Killer*. Delish. https://www.delish.com/cooking/recipe-ideas/a19664658/best-turkey-burger-recipe/

Hillyer, L. (2016, July). *Sausage Veggie Grill*. Taste of Home. https://www.tasteofhome.com/recipes/sausage-veggie-grill/

Jenn. (2019, December 7). *Chicken Sausage Egg Bites*. A Dash of Macros. https://adashofmacros.com/chicken-sausage-egg-bites/

Julia. (2018, July 28). *Grilled Turkey Kabobs*. Happy Foods Tube. https://www.happyfoodstube.com/grilled-turkey-kabobs/

Kirk, K., & Kirk, R. (2016, June 7). *Mojo Marinated Grilled Chicken*. Laughing Spatula. https://laughingspatula.com/mojo-marinated-grilled-chicken/

Mikesell, D. (2021, May 13). *Grilled Turkey Breast from 101 Cooking for Two*. 101 Cooking for Two. https://www.101cookingfortwo.com/grilled-brown-sugar-rubbed-turkey/

Oven-Roasted Turkey Drumsticks – trumacro Nutrition. (n.d.). Trumacro. Retrieved September 24, 2021, from https://trumacro.com/keto-turkey-drumsticks/

Denny, K. (2018, August 7). *Marinated Pork Chops with Soy Sauce, Cumin, Lime, and Oregano*. Kalyn's Kitchen. https://kalynskitchen.com/grilled-pork-chops-recipe-with-soy/

Georgina, A. (2017, March 28). *Easy Spiced Pork Chops*. Step Away from the Carbs. https://stepawayfromthecarbs.com/easy-spiced-pork-chops/

Gerri. (2019, November 2). *Keto Pepper Pork Stew - Creamy Low Carb Slow Cooker Recipe*. My Keto Kitchen. https://www.myketokitchen.com/keto-recipes/keto-pepper-pork-stew/

Grilled Keto Pork Tenderloin Recipe. (2020, January 22). Don't Sweat the Recipe. https://www.dontsweattherecipe.com/the-best-keto-grilled-pork-tenderloin-recipe/

Jenn. (2020, April 20). *Pork Shoulder Green Chili Stew*. A Dash of Macros. https://adashofmacros.com/pork-shoulder-green-chili-stew/

Kathleen. (2020, October 31). *Pork Stew (One Pot Comfort Food!)*. Gonna Want Seconds. https://www.gonnawantseconds.com/pork-stew/#wprm-recipe-container-23870

Kitchen, P. (2005, February 24). *Baked Pork Chops with Potatoes and Gravy*. Pillsbury.com. https://www.pillsbury.com/recipes/baked-pork-chops-with-potatoes-and-gravy/d9e8d6cd-f045-44ab-98dc-390f4b195d25?int=td&rc=pork&gclid=CjwKCAjw7rWKBhAtEiwAJ3CWLLgIXHNUBmwkDgr0Rt2MRw4sU2UrJE7KB41v0Ti3Y94pY3faNWxFmx0Cr7QQAvD_BwE

Manager, C. (n.d.). *Carb Manager*. Carb Manager. Retrieved September 24, 2021, from https://www.carbmanager.com/recipe-detail/ug:508497e8-8f9e-b4e9-63f6-4ebe26d884a7/keto-pulled-pork-stew

March 12, J. •, & Comments, 2020 524. (2021, August 30). *The Best Juicy Skillet Pork Chops*. Inspired Taste - Easy Recipes for Home Cooks. https://www.inspiredtaste.net/37062/juicy-skillet-pork-chops/

Maxwell, K. (2019, December 20). *Pan Roasted Pork Loin*. Yellow Bliss Road. https://www.yellowblissroad.com/pan-roasted-pork-loin/

Melissa. (2018, May 23). *Keto Pork Chops al Pastor - Low Carb*. I Breathe I'm Hungry. https://www.ibreatheimhungry.com/keto-pork-chops-al-pastor-low-carb/

Olivia. (2021, May 11). *Garlic Butter Baked Pork Chops*. Primavera Kitchen. https://www.primaverakitchen.com/garlic-butter-baked-pork-chops/

Pork Chops. (2017, August 22). Delish. https://www.delish.com/cooking/recipe-ideas/recipes/a54981/pan-fried-pork-chop-recipe/

Rich Pork Stew Recipe with Root Vegetables. (2020, July 22). Scrambled Chefs. https://www.scrambledchefs.com/rich-pork-stew-recipe-with-root-vegetables/

Steamy Kitchen Hungarian Pork Stew Recipe Macro Nutrition Facts. (n.d.). Ketofoodist.com. Retrieved September 24, 2021, from https://ketofoodist.com/recipe/43170082/

Keto Flank Steak - Low Carb, Gluten Free. (2020, August 8). Kicking Carbs. https://kicking-carbs.com/keto-flank-steak/

Low Carb Keto Beef Kabobs. (2018, August 9). Noshtastic. https://www.noshtastic.com/low-carb-keto-beef-kabobs/

says, M. P. P.-M. M. T. (2016, January 28). *Pot Roast*. GetMacroEd. https://getmacroed.com/pot-roast/

Pictures from: https://unsplash.com/

Ann. (2020, February 25). *The Best Vegan Stew*. Our Happy Mess. https://www.ourhappymess.com/vegan-stew/

Holly. (2019, August 3). *Garlic Grilled Shrimp*. Spend with Pennies. https://www.spendwithpennies.com/garlic-grilled-shrimp/

Holly. (2020, January 1). *Weight Loss Vegetable Soup {with Amazing Flavor}*. Spend with Pennies. https://www.spendwithpennies.com/weight-loss-vegetable-soup-recipe/

Liz. (2021, March 2). *Vegan Beef Stew*. ZardyPlants. https://zardyplants.com/recipes/vegan-beef-stew/

Made in the USA
Columbia, SC
12 May 2025